ANATOMY
—OF A GARDEN—

PETER McHOY

WINDWARD

Editor: Susanne Mitchell
Designer: Glynis Edwards
Picture research: Moira McIlroy
Production: Richard Churchill

Published by Windward
an imprint owned by W. H. Smith & Son Limited
Registered No. 237811 England
Trading as WHS Distributors,
St John's House, East Street, Leicester LE1 6NE

© Marshall Cavendish Limited 1987

ISBN 0 7112 04632

Typeset in Novarese by Tradespools, Frome,
England
Printed and bound in Hong Kong

Contents

Introduction

Successful gardening is a result of many things – a promising site, satisfactory soil, an understanding of plants and how they grow, a little imagination and a touch of the artist's flair for knowing what looks right together . . . even a little luck. You can't always arrange these things, but understanding the anatomy of a garden, what plants need and how they fit into the garden, will almost certainly bring you more success.

Taking stock of the garden

This book is partly about growing better plants, and partly about integrating them within the garden. If you are taking over an existing garden or renovating a neglected one this may involve a degree of redesigning as no amount of replanting will overcome fundamental design defects. If you do have to reconstruct part of the garden, establishing priorities for the work involved is important.

Start by retaining as many existing plants as possible – obviously it is best to leave them where they are, but consider trying to move them if this is not feasible (see page 84). With a large plant you may have to make preparations to do this six months or more in advance.

If new plants are needed, concentrate on choosing the trees and shrubs first. These take the longest to mature. You can help to create an established impression by planting quick-growing trees and shrubs (see page 105), but you will almost certainly want to include some slow-growing plants too.

However large or small your garden, whatever plants it contains, it will have shortcomings. There will be plants that don't grow well, plants that seem to be in the wrong place, plants you see growing so well in other peoples' gardens that just won't seem to grow in

There is no need to spend a lot of money on elaborate garden features in order to have an attractive garden. A colourful mix of plants is always effective.

yours. Fortunately there will almost certainly be plants that do thrive, groupings that look really good in your garden, features that give it an individual character. Take a critical look at your garden – capitalise on its strengths, and then see what you can do about its weaknesses – not only by the choice of plants, but also by improving the soil, providing windbreaks, or maybe by the careful use of screens and windbreaks.

This book has been written with the intention of providing the help and advice you need in order to do this. *The Anatomy of a Garden* is intended for those gardeners who want to know how to create a better garden by understanding the principles of gardening. But it is not just a theoretical book; throughout the text the principles have been related to practical jobs, and it should be as useful to the complete beginner who wants to make a better garden but does not know how, as to the experienced gardener who simply wants to know more about modern techniques or who is looking for more ideas to use plants creatively.

In the first two chapters you will find lots of useful information on the soil and climate – how to get the better of it, or at least come to terms with it. It will help you to choose the plants that should grow well.

There is a chapter on growing and caring for your plants: how to get them off to a good start, and to keep them growing happily, how to prune and train

plants . . . and how to propagate them when you want more. Because it deals with the principles, as well as advice for specific plants, you should be able to cope successfully with most of the plants in your garden.

A collection of well-grown plants does not necessarily make a well-designed or attractive garden. The right plants need to be in the right place, in a happy association with their neighbours. There is advice on choosing plants to form the framework of the garden, and those to clothe it with form and texture. Again the principles can be applied to plants however obscure or exotic, but there are also plenty of suggested plants that are easy to obtain as well as dependable and easy to grow.

If you are not familiar with all the Latin names of plants mentioned in the book, use the common name index. There the common names are cross-referenced to their Latin equivalents.

Nobody wants their efforts spoilt by pests or diseases, nor does one want a constant battle with weeds. The last chapter will help you to get the better of these problems – without necessarily always reaching for garden chemicals first.

There can be no blueprint for an ideal garden – fortunately each one is different – but whatever its size, its shape, its soil, there will be plenty of scope. This book should help you to realize it through an appreciation of the principles of gardening.

The Soil

Soil is frequently taken for granted — until you have to dig it. Yet it is a complex structure and the interactions of the various physical, chemical and biological processes that go on within it affect the way plants will grow. It is the life-support system of the garden.

What is Soil?

Whether you have an established garden or are starting from scratch with a bare plot of land, it is worth spending some time getting to know your soil. Although the ground in which the plants grow is often ignored and neglected, it is usually the biggest single reason for success or failure. A good gardener will take as much care of the life under the surface as he will the life on it.

Soil has five major constituents: mineral matter (derived from the breakdown of underlying rocks or gravel), humus (from decaying plants and animal material), water (which contains organic and inorganic substances in solution), air, and many forms of plant and animal life.

Soil is not a solid mass, about half its volume is made up of inorganic soil particles, the rest is composed of spaces, the small ones usually filled with water, the larger ones with air. The solid particles are coated with a jelly of mineral and organic substances. And the temperature is neither so hot in summer nor so cold in winter as the outside air. All the normal conditions for normal life are there with the exception of light.

Structure and Texture

There are many ways of classifying the structure and texture of soils, but they

Whatever your soil, there will be plants that will thrive. These are growing on a light, sandy, acid soil.

all depend on assessing the proportion of sand, silt and clay particles that the soil contains.

Most soils are a combination of all three, and it is the relative proportions of each that give a soil its characteristic texture, its water-holding capacity and, to some extent, its capacity for retaining nutrients. *Sand* particles are irregular in shape and do not compact together closely; because there are relatively large air gaps between the particles, soils in which sand predominates can be dug easily and are generally referred to as *'light'* soils. Light soils warm up quickly in spring but they also drain rapidly in periods of drought.

Clay particles are very small and, as there is little air between them, they are packed together more densely. This makes soils in which clay particles predominate difficult to dig and heavy to lift, and for that reason they are known as *'heavy'* soils. These soils hold moisture readily.

Clay particles, however, contribute the most to soil fertility. Because of their small size they give the soil a large surface area upon which chemical reactions can take place, but they also have interesting physical properties too. They stick together when wet (which is why clay soils are so sticky and difficult to dig when wet), but when they dry the mass becomes hard and shrinks so that cracks may form, see illustration page 23.

Silt particles are intermediate in size between the large sand grains and the tiny clay particles.

Silt particles, like sand, are inert and therefore provide little food for plants or other members of the soil population. By blocking up the pore spaces between the particles of sand they can impede drainage.

Both sands and silts contribute much to the *structure* of the soil but little to its chemical reactivity. A predominantly sandy soil usually lacks nutrients.

The Importance of Air in the Soil

Air, particularly its oxygen content, is necessary for the roots of most plants (waterlogged soil will quickly kill many plants, although aquatic and bog plants are an exception), and for most soil inhabitants to survive. The amount of air present in the soil depends on the amount of water present as well as upon the soil structure itself. Despite the seemingly solid appearance of soil, it has been estimated that air in the soil to a depth of about 13 cm (5 in) is completely renewed every hour. No matter how small the cracks and pores, molecules of oxygen, for example, are very much smaller.

Earthworms and soil insects can help soil aeration by making passages in the soil, and on heavy clay soils the cracks that form when they dry also help.

What is Humus?

Humus is something much talked about in gardening circles, but quite difficult to visualize and describe. It is the slowly decomposing residues of organic matter (plants and animals), which form a black colloidal material that coats the soil particles. Its role in soil fertility is crucially important. The humus coating on the soil particles has a high cation exchange capacity (which means that more nutrients are held by the humus ready to be absorbed by the plants). Clay has this capacity anyway, but sandy soils lack it – so humus is very important for sandy soils. But humus helps clay soils in another way – it adheres strongly to the particles and helps to create a good crumb structure. This in turn makes the soil more 'workable'.

Humus will gradually diminish as it is decomposed by bacteria, so it has to be replaced regularly (in nature by fallen leaves and rotting vegetation, in the garden by adding some form of bulky organic matter).

Crumb Structure

The various particles in soil are grouped together into 'crumbs' of up to about 3 mm (⅛ in) in diameter – if you crush a small clod of dryish garden soil you will see that it breaks up into crumbs. The soil is likely to have a more pronounced crumb structure where plants, especially grasses, have been growing. The crumb structure is important; if the finest particles are held in crumbs, rainwater can more easily seep down to the lower depths. And because the crumbs are irregular in shape, there is more space for air to circulate.

Some crumbs are relatively unstable and break down in heavy rain for instance; if the ground is dug or cultivated when it's too wet much of the crumb structure is lost, making it sticky and unfavourable to plant roots. If just the surface layer crumbs break down the soil forms a 'cap' which reduces the ability of moisture and air to penetrate the soil, and makes it more difficult for seeds to germinate.

Humus helps the soil particles to form crumbs, and this is one reason why the addition of plenty of organic material such as garden compost and bulky manures helps to improve soil structure.

Topsoil and Subsoil

To inspect the nature of the soil, dig one or more trial holes about 45 cm (18 in) deep. There will almost certainly be fairly clearly defined layers that are obvious to the eye. The uppermost layer (topsoil) is darker, looser, and more crumb-like in structure (though if you have a new garden on clay this may not be very obvious). The topsoil is seldom more than 15–30 cm (6–12 in) deep because that is the depth where most of the roots are, and the depth to which worms and other soil creatures can take plant residues. It will probably have received dressing of manures and fertilizers, or will at least have benefited from natural rotting vegetation.

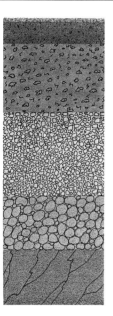   

Far left This artist's impression shows how a typical soil overlying rock may be composed of bands of stone, gravel, subsoil, and a relatively shallow layer of topsoil.
Centre left Clay soils are often poorly aerated and badly drained, as well as difficult to dig.
Centre right Sandy soils are easy to dig and cultivate, but water drains quickly through the top layers, often washing away nutrients at the same time. The plants may suffer from drought and nutritional deficiencies.
Right A good loam is a mixture of sand, clay, and humus. It is easy to cultivate.

This is the fertile layer, with the best soil structure and the greatest reserve of nutrients. It is for that reason that any form of cultivation should not bring too much of the next layer – the subsoil – to the top (see Digging).

Although the underlying layer – the subsoil – is less fertile it is still important. It is often lighter in colour and stickier in texture.

If underlying rock is close to the surface, the shallowness of the soil may mean that trees are more likely to blow down and drought may be more of a problem. More importantly, the underlying rocks can affect the alkalinity of the soil.

Assessing Your Soil

Start by determining the *type* of soil that you have. If you have been cultivating it for some time, you will probably know already whether it is predominantly clay (heavy) or sandy (light), but there are other types between these extremes that are less easy to determine.

There are no simple tests that will tell you how rich your soil is in nutrients, or if it is acid or alkaline, simply by appearance or touch. If you want a full soil analysis it is best to have a professional soil test done, although pH tests are easy to do yourself.

Acidity and Alkalinity
The level of acidity or alkalinity of a soil is measured on what is called a pH scale. The pH is of importance not only to a wide range of plants that have preferences for either acid or alkaline soils, but also for nutrient availability.

On the pH scale, 7 is technically neutral; values less than this are acid, values greater are alkaline. In temperate areas most soils lie within the range 5.5 to 7.5, and are only rarely as low as 4 or as high as 8.

pH affects the growth of plants, and also the occurrence of pest and dis-

---

Identify Your Soil Type

As a guide to the main soil types try the following test. Take a small handful of soil from a few inches below the surface, and if it is very dry moisten it slightly, kneading it between the fingers and thumb.

● If it feels predominantly rough and gritty and trickles easily between the fingers, it will contain a high percentage of sand. This will be a light soil, which will drain easily, warm up early and may well be deficient in nutrients.

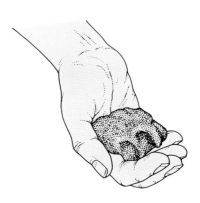

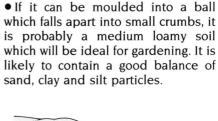

● If it moulds into a strong ball that smears across the fingers, then the soil contains a high percentage of clay and silt. This will be a heavy soil, slow to warm up and not draining readily. Depending on the level of clay, it will be difficult to work.

● If it can be moulded into a ball which falls apart into small crumbs, it is probably a medium loamy soil which will be ideal for gardening. It is likely to contain a good balance of sand, clay and silt particles.

---

eases, as well as many soil organisms. Most plants grow best within a pH range of about 6.5 to 7.5, although some prefer more acid or alkaline conditions. Cucumbers, parsley, and tomatoes do best between 5.5 and 6.5, mushrooms between 7 and 8, for example.

Some popular flowers require an acid soil unless you take steps to combat mineral deficiencies induced by too much lime – see page 19. Azaleas,

camellias, heathers, and rhododendrons are examples. These are known as *calcifuges* (those that tolerate a high pH well are called *calcicoles*).

Soil pH also affects the availability of nutrients (see page 14), but most of them are readily available to plants at 6.5. This is probably one reason why most plants do best on a slightly acid soil. On peaty soils, however, 5.8 seems to be the optimum.

Testing for pH

The techniques vary slightly with the type of kit being used, but start by taking samples from the top 5–8 cm (2–3 in) of soil with a clean spoon and spread them out on a saucer to dry out a little if they are very wet. Remove any stones or fibrous material.

Most kits use an indicator fluid which is added to a soil solution and the resulting colour compared against a chart. You will have to put an amount of the soil into a test tube, and pour on the correct quantity of indicator solution. The test tube is corked and shaken vigorously then allowed to stand upright for about 10 minutes, by which time the liquid should have cleared enough to be compared with the colour guide provided. The pH of the soil is read from the colour guide.

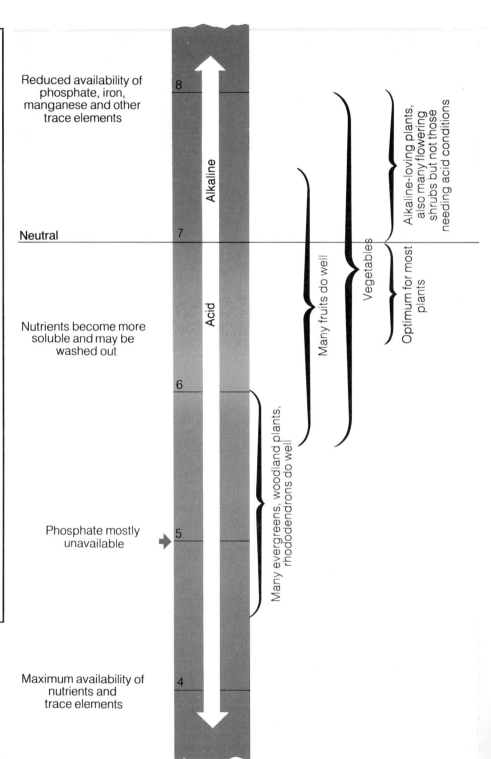

Reduced availability of phosphate, iron, manganese and other trace elements

Neutral

Alkaline

8

7

Acid

6

Nutrients become more soluble and may be washed out

Phosphate mostly unavailable

5

Maximum availability of nutrients and trace elements

4

Many evergreens, woodland plants, rhododendrons do well

Many fruits do well

Vegetables

Optimum for most plants

Alkaline-loving plants, also many flowering shrubs but not those needing acid conditions

The pH scale

Adjusting the pH

It is much easier to make your soil more alkaline than it is to make it more acid, but significant adjustments are possible in either direction. If you hope to achieve a really big change however (say to grow acid-lovers such as rhododendrons and azaleas on a naturally alkaline soil; or to grow lime-lovers on a very acid soil), it is more practical and more satisfactory to grow the 'difficult' plants in containers or in raised beds. Better still, whenever possible grow those plants that are naturally adapted to your type of soil.

Often, however, it is both desirable and practicable to adjust the pH, and the following advice should enable you to make reasonably accurate adjustments, although every soil will react differently.

MAKING YOUR SOIL MORE ALKALINE

As a guide, the following amount of lime should be applied to increase alkalinity by 1 pH.

Soil type	Hydrated lime	Ground limestone
Clay	640 g/sq m (18 oz/sq yd)	850 g/sq m (24 oz/sq yd)
Average loam	410 g/sq m (12 oz/sq yd)	550 g/sq m (16 oz/sq yd)
Sand	200 g/sq m (6 oz/sq yd)	275 g/sq m (8 oz/sq yd)

Test the soil again after a month to see whether further adjustment is necessary. Once the desired pH has been reached it should not be necessary to apply more lime for several years – perhaps for two or three years on a sandy soil, longer on a clay soil. In areas of high rainfall, it may be necessary to lime more frequently than in areas with average or low rainfall.

MAKING YOUR SOIL MORE ACID

The following should increase soil acidity by 1 pH, but bear in mind that sulphate of ammonia is a nitrogenous fertilizer, and too much of it could affect the balance of plant growth.

Sulphate of ammonia	70 g/sq m (2½ oz/sq yd)
Flowers of sulphur	70 g/sq m (2½ oz/sq yd)
Peat	1.5 kg/sq m (3 lb/sq yd)
Garden compost	9 kg/sq m (20 lb/sq yd)
Manure	3 kg/sq m (6 lb/sq yd)

The colour of many hydrangea flowers is affected by the acidity or alkalinity of the soil – something to bear in mind when you buy a hydrangea. These pictures of 'Wonder' are taken in the same garden, the one on the left was growing in acid soil, the one on the right in alkaline soil.

What is Lime?

Lime is the popular name for the oxides and carbonates of the element calcium. Lime in nature occurs mainly in the form of accumulated deposits of primitive animal shells.

When limestone or chalk is burnt in a kiln, the carbon dioxide is driven off, leaving pure calcium oxide – quicklime. This is unsuitable for garden use so it is slaked with water to produce hydrated lime – which is easy to store and handle, and is non-caustic.

Ground limestone is the unburned raw material ground into a fairly fine powder. This is the form in which lime is usually added to the other ingredients of potting composts.

Applying lime

The various limes are evaluated on their calcium-oxide content, and this accounts for the need to apply much more of some forms of lime than of others – something to take into account when working out comparative cost.

The amount of lime required also depends to some extent on the type of soil. A sandy soil requires only half as much as a heavy soil to achieve the same degree of saturation and to cure the same degree of acidity. If you apply the same amount to a light soil as is necessary to correct a deficiency on a heavy soil, you will probably induce deficiencies of trace elements.

The amount of water held by the soil is crucial for healthy plant growth. The ideal amount is when the soil is at 'field capacity' (centre), when it is holding as much moisture as it can against the force of gravity. Water surrounds all the soil particles, and small pore spaces are filled, but air is available in the pores between the large particles. When the soil is saturated or waterlogged (left), there are no air spaces and most plants will die if this condition lasts for long; when the permanent wilting point is reached (right), what little moisture is present is held too tightly to be available to the plants.

Testing for Nutrients

A pH test will only tell you how much lime you need to apply (or if the soil is too alkaline by what extent you may need to make it more acid). Although plants need calcium, the lime that you apply will primarily be to adjust acidity. If you want to know which plant foods might be necessary, you will have to buy a NPK kit (N = nitrogen; P = phosphorus; K = potassium). These three elements are the major plant nutrients, and the ones most likely to be deficient (see page 68).

For all these elements a proper laboratory analysis is best, but as your garden may vary considerably from one part to the next, especially if various areas have been growing different plants with different treatments, there are attractions in using DIY kits.

An amateur NPK test kit is likely to contain indicator solutions like a pH kit, and most of the tests are made in a similar way, the colour of the sample solution being compared with a card that will indicate a probable percentage deficiency.

If you do not want to bother with a full soil analysis, you will not go far wrong by testing the pH, adjusting that if

necessary, and applying a generally balanced fertilizer (see page 28) each spring as routine.

Deficiencies of the minor nutrients are a problem on some soils, but these will make themselves known by their effect on plant growth (see page 68). Some are easily corrected, but others have to be applied in a special form if the deficiency is induced by a high pH for instance. This is another reason for measuring the pH and trying to deal with any extremes, as this could explain some of the nutrient deficiencies.

Water in the Soil

The water-holding capacity of the soil, and ways of keeping it at an optimum level, are very important as too much or too little water can both be limiting factors to plant growth. Soil micro-organisms are also dependent on water for their existence. Ideally there should be sufficient small pores in the soil to hold water, and sufficient large pores to allow water to drain freely and allow a free exchange of gases.

If the large pore spaces in the soil are filled with water, the soil is saturated. Only specially adapted plants will live long in these conditions as the water excludes the oxygen that forms an important part of the gaseous exchange between roots and soil. The ideal amount of soil moisture for most plants is when the soil is holding as much as it can against the pull of gravity. This is known as *field capacity* and at this point the pores are surrounded by a film of water, the small spaces are filled with water but there is air in the larger pores. Although gravity is unable to pull the remaining water from the pores, the plant roots can – for a time anyway. There comes a point, however, when the water is retained so firmly by the soil particles that roots can no longer extract it and this is known as the *permanent wilting point*.

Improving the Moisture-holding Capacity

The best way of improving the moisture-holding capacity of any soil, while retaining sufficient air spaces, is by improving soil structure: forming a better crumb structure in clay soils and increasing the humus content of sandy soils. This can be done by adding plenty of organic material.

There are other materials which will help in retaining water – peat is a traditional one – and there are man-made superabsorbent polymers that will hold water so that it is available to the plant roots (though in the garden these are used primarily for containers that are likely to dry out quickly). Vermiculite and perlite combine good water retention with good aeration. But none of these is really a practical or economic solution on a large scale in the garden, though they are very useful for pot or container-grown plants.

Mulching will help to reduce water loss by evaporation from the soil (see page 31), but sooner or later most plants will benefit from irrigation.

Soil Temperature

Soil temperature is sometimes a more critical factor than air temperature (see seed sowing, page 44). Certainly if you are sowing seeds outdoors you should be guided by the soil temperature rather than the calendar or the more transient air temperature on a particular day.

The soil will warm up and cool down more slowly than the air, so there is a buffering effect that evens out some of the wide variations of air temperature. But temperature will depend on the soil depth at which you take it, as well as the position within the garden.

Some plants, such as Iris laevigata, *are specially adapted and can grow in waterlogged conditions. Others, like hostas, will grow in moist soil.*

A wet soil requires more than twice as much heat as a dry one to raise its temperature through a given range, so not all soils warm up at the same rate. For that reason you may have to delay sowing on a wet soil. On the other hand, the temperature of wet soil is less likely to drop so dramatically at night.

A light soil warms up more quickly in spring than a heavy soil and cloches placed in position a few weeks before sowing will also bring about an increase in soil temperature.

Wilting

Wilting is often a sign that a plant needs water – but not always. It may simply be that the plant is not able to transport enough water to the leaves to compensate for losses through the leaf pores, and once the temperature cools at night the plant recovers. This is temporary wilting.

An earthworm, Lumbricus terrestris, *one of several species that you will find in the garden. Although cast-forming species can be a nuisance on a quality lawn, earthworms are generally to be welcomed as they help to improve soil structure and fertility.*

Soil Inhabitants

The soil is home for a vast population of microscopic life forms as well as the more obvious insects, spiders, mites and worms.

Invisible Inhabitants

The most important of the microscopic life in the soil are the bacteria which, despite their size, play a crucial role in soil fertility and plant growth. Although some bacteria are harmful, many are extremely beneficial and break down a large number of organic and inorganic residues into a form which can be assimilated by the plant. Some bacteria convert nitrogen from the atmosphere into a form that is available to plants. These bacteria live in nodules on the roots of peas, beans, clover and related plants (known as legumes) and this is the reason why it is beneficial to leave the roots of leguminous plants in the ground.

Soil Fungi

These include moulds, mildews, mushrooms as well as other forms. Some are large and very visible, others are not invisible to the naked eye but generally work unseen beneath the ground. Others – including many plant diseases – are small enough to live within the plant. Once again, some are beneficial, others are not.

Other Inhabitants

Other inhabitants include algae, lichens, and soil protozoa. And there are even viruses that kill bacteria and which may be a hundred times smaller than small bacteria. Particular viruses can usually attack only specific bacteria. The soil, especially within the air spaces, is home for many creatures.

A large number of insects and other arthropods (arthropods include woodlice, mites, millipedes, and symphilids) are found in soil. Some of those that are

Earthworms

These are, perhaps, the best-known soil inhabitants. Generally, earthworms should be encouraged as they are a sign of fertile land with plenty of organic matter. Soil with very few worms is likely to be a problem.

Not all worms are cast-makers, in fact only two regularly leave casts on the surface. But as a result of this, fine soil material, which has passed through the gut of the worms, is brought to the surface, while leaves and other organic material is taken beneath the surface. The burrowing activities of earthworms also help aeration and drainage. They burrow partly by pushing between cracks and partly by eating some of the soil.

Although some species live in the surface layers of the soil, others burrow down – sometimes as much as

2 m (6½ ft) though this is exceptional.

The earthworm population and activity is affected by soil pH, moisture, temperature, and the amount of organic matter that it contains.

Generally, worms prefer soils with good reserves of calcium, and they tend to be more abundant on alkaline soil than on acid soil. The absence of plenty of organic matter generally means a relative absence of earthworms too. Where there is plenty of organic material, such as a compost or manure heap, there will be plenty of worms.

The earthworm population will also drop when the soil is cultivated. This is because there is likely to be less reserves of humus, and the digging disturbs the worms and exposes them to predators.

pests are described on page 132. Those that are not pests you can ignore. Always bear in mind that some can be beneficial (see page 131).

Nematodes (usually known to gardeners as eelworms) are small thread-like worms. Some are free-living, and even beneficial; although they are usually found near plant roots many feed on bacteria, small algae, protozoa, and even other nematodes. Some others, however, are parasitic and live on plants and are a serious problem for gardeners. Some species can form cysts that can remain in a dormant state for several years, only to be activated again when the right host comes along. The horticulturally important types are mentioned on page 132.

Chalk Soils

If you garden on an alkaline soil there will be some plants that you cannot grow well unless you make special provision for them, but these will be comparatively few.

You will have problems if you try to grow acid-loving plants but there are so many others that will thrive there is little point in struggling with these.

Improving the Soil
You can reduce the pH as described on page 15, but these measures are best reserved for fairly small areas where you particularly want to grow plants that would otherwise be difficult.

Some of the remedies are also expensive if applied to a large area and peat, for example, could be used much more economically by getting plants off to a good start: incorporate plenty into the planting hole, and mulch with moist peat (moss peat is likely to be more acid than sedge peat). If using flowers of sulphur, be prepared to use it twice a year until the required level is reached – and bear in mind that simply altering the pH of the top few inches will not

Why Chalk Soils Can be a Problem

Lime-hating plants often have yellow, sickly leaves if grown on alkaline soil – a sign of chlorosis caused by a lack of iron that is vital for the production of chlorophyll, which is what gives leaves their green colour. Although there may be plenty of iron in the soil, the high pH locks it up in a form unavailable to the plant.

Plants that *prefer* an alkaline soil may have become adapted to grow best with the lower nutrient levels associated with this type of soil. Plants that thrive on chalk have a more efficient mechanism for converting the iron locked up in the soil into a form in which it can be absorbed by the roots.

The vast majority of plants that grow in a neutral soil will also grow satisfactorily in alkaline soils too, even though they might not do quite so well.

have much effect on established plants with their roots deeper into the soil.

Apply plenty of organic matter to improve moisture-retention and soil structure as well as to modify the pH. You will need plenty of it applied regularly, as the high pH favours many of the micro-organisms that break down organic matter quickly.

Do not use mushroom compost to provide the organic material, as it is likely to have a high pH itself.

Do whatever you can to increase the depth of fertile soil if it is shallow. Double digging will help and regular mulching will gradually increase the soil depth, while at the same time providing humus and reducing water loss.

Feeding
To supply the major nutrients use a normal balanced fertilizer. If a nitrogenous fertilizer is needed, use an acid

one like sulphate of ammonia and not the alkaline Nitro-chalk.

The nutrients most likely to be deficient on an alkaline soil are the trace elements manganese and iron (see page 68 for symptoms). Simply adding these as chemicals to the soil may not help as the soil alters them so that they cannot be absorbed by the plant's roots. They can, however, be applied as chelated compounds that remain stable in the soil and available to the plants for many months. These compounds may be sold as Sequestrene, and some contain all the elements likely to be deficient due to a high soil pH. Apply according to maker's instructions.

Foliar feeding is another option, but more of a chore. Use a suitable soluble feed, and apply it when the weather is dull, perhaps in the evening, to reduce the risk of scorching, and to give the plants more chance to absorb the nutrients before it evaporates.

Gardening on Clay

There are simple tests you can try to determine what kind of soil you have (see page 13), and if you think it is clay try the following test to confirm it.

Try to mould the soil ball (moisten the soil a little if it is dry), before rolling it into a sausage and bending it round to form a ring. If it will not stick together easily and cannot easily be rolled into a sausage, it has probably got a clay content of less than 35 per cent and there is no special problem. Once the clay content reaches about 40 per cent it will roll into a sausage easily, and it can be bent into a ring without fracturing. The higher the clay content, the longer the sausages that you will be able to produce easily, and the tighter the rings that you can make.

Clay soils often grow very good plants. They are not likely to be especially deficient in nutrients, and established plants are likely to do very well. They are, however, exceedingly difficult to cultivate. Digging is especially hard work, and even hoeing can need more effort. Anything newly planted will suffer if the ground dries out and cracks, or conversely becomes too wet and waterlogged. Getting a fine tilth to sow seeds is a particular problem. For this reason a clay soil can make a vegetable garden very difficult to work, and rootcrops are often disappointing.

Clay soils are also slow to warm up in spring and plants with fine fibrous root systems suffer from the poor soil aeration in winter and from drought during the summer.

For all these reasons it is worth trying to improve your soil if the clay content is high, though if the garden is large or resources restricted, it is best to concentrate efforts in a comparatively small area (say the vegetable garden, or some important ornamental beds), rather than to try to improve the whole garden and have little overall impact. For the

---

Some Plants to Avoid

Unless you are prepared to grow them in containers, or to make special planting pits or raised beds, it is best to avoid the following plants on chalky soils:

Acer japonicum, A. palmatum,
 A. rubrum
Azaleas
Callunas (heather)
Camellias
Clethra
Cornus florida, C. kousa, C. nuttallii
Corylopsis pauciflora
Crinodendron hookeranum
Cytisus scoparius (broom)
Daboecia
Enkianthus
Erica (though E. x darleyensis, E. herbacea,
 syn. E. carnea, and E. mediterranea usually
 tolerate chalk well)
Escallonia (some)
Eucryphia
Fothergilla monticola

Gaultheria
Gentians (most, though there are some
 important exceptions such as G. acaulis
 and G. septemfida that do well on chalky
 soils)
Halesia
Kalmia
Lilium auratum, L. giganteum (syn.
 Cardiocrinum giganteum), L. japonicum, L.
 speciosum, L. tigrinum
Liquidambar styraciflua
Lithospermum diffusum
Lupinus (except L. arboreus)
Magnolia (most)
Meconopsis (most, but not M. cambrica)
Nyssa
Pachysandra terminalis
Pernettya
Pieris
Primula japonica
Rhododendron
Skimmia reevesiana
Ulex
Vaccinium

areas that you cannot tackle, concentrate on perennials such as shrubs, choosing those that you know will thrive on clay. Some are suggested here.

Cultivating Clay

It is especially important to cultivate clay soils at the right time. If you walk on them when they are too wet the compaction will make matters worse. Try to avoid walking on the soil as much as possible, and certainly when it is very wet. Dig it in the autumn (ideally when the ground is moist but not too wet) and leave it rough-dug over the winter if possible.

Digging can be made easier by using a fork whenever possible, but if you have to use a spade, dipping it into a bucket of water after each spadeful may help it to slide through the soil more easily. If you have to dig when the soil is wet, try standing on a plank to spread your weight.

Improving Clay

Improving clay soils involves getting the very small particles to form small lumps or crumbs. Digging to expose the soil to frost, and the action of worms and plant roots, will help to improve the crumb structure. The addition of a lot of organic matter will help by chemically binding the soil into crumbs.

When you break the rough-dug soil down in spring, fork in as much garden compost, manure, or other bulky organic manures as you can spare. This will not achieve instant or permanent results, but it will improve the structure steadily over the years if done annually.

The addition of sand can be a cheap and convenient method, but use sharp sand, not builder's soft sand. Even small gravel may help, as will chemically inert products like expanded clay granules and expanded volcanic ash, as these all have a physical effect on soil structure. The problem is one of amount and cost – you will probably have to add about 10 per cent by bulk

Recommended Plants for Clay Soil

SHRUBS
Abelia
Amelanchier
Arundinaria
Aucuba japonica
Berberis
Buddleia davidii
Buxus
Chaenomeles
Choisya ternata
Cornus alba, C. mas,
C. stolonifera
Corylus avellana, C. maximus
'Purpureus'
Cotinus coggygria
Cotoneaster
Cytisus
Deutzia
Elaeagnus × ebbingei,
E. pungens
Enkianthus campanulatus
Escallonia
Euonymus
Forsythia
Fothergilla major
Genista
Hamamelis
Hebe
Hibiscus syriacus
Hydrangea
Hypericum
Ilex
Kerria japonica
Ligustrum
Lonicera
Mahonia
Magnolia
Osmanthus
Pernettya mucronata
Philadelphus
Phyllostachys
Potentilla
Prunus 'Cistena', *P. incisa,*
P. laurocerasus, P. tenella
Pyracantha
Rhododendron
(if soil is acid)
Rhus typhina
Ribes
Rosa
Rubus
Salix

Sambucus
Sarcococca
Senecio 'Sunshine'
(may be sold as S. *greyi* or
S. *laxifolius*)
Skimmia
Sorbus
Spiraea
Symphoricarpos
Syringa vulgaris
Viburnum
Vinca
Weigela

HERBACEOUS PLANTS
Achillea
Aconitum
Anchusa
Aquilegia
Aruncus sylvester

Bergenia
Campanula lactiflora
Digitalis
Geranium
Geum
Helleborus
Hemerocallis
Hosta
Lysimachia
Lythrum
Narcissus
(including daffodils)
Papaver
Primula (many,
including polyanthus)
Rudbeckia
Snowdrop
Tradescantia
Trollius
Viola

Deutzia 'Magician', a good shrub for clay soils

Laying Drains

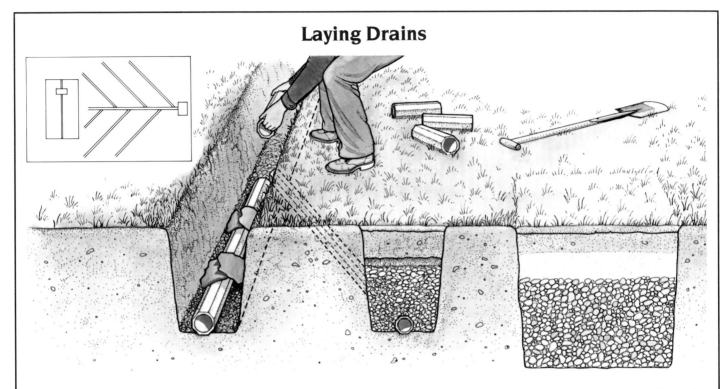

If you are not sure whether drainage is a problem, dig some 30 cm (1 ft) holes at various points in the garden shortly after heavy rain. If after a few hours there is a quantity of water in the holes, drainage will probably be beneficial; the more water there is, the more worthwhile it is likely to be.

The illustrations show how drains are laid. Whatever type of drain is used, lay them with a slight fall, leading to a soakaway if there is no natural outlet such as a ditch or an area that you can use as, say, a bog garden. Always make sure the water drains away from the house (but avoid simply taking the water into a neighbour's garden!). The soakaway (or dry well) should be at least 1.2m (4ft) deep and filled with aggregate and gravel. Land drains are available from builders' merchants.

to make a real impact. However, this might be feasible for a small area.

You may want to do something about drainage if this is a problem, though any drainage system involves hard work as well as expense, and laying such a system in an established garden can scar it too, so you would only want to do this if it is really necessary. If you are in doubt, see 'Laying Drains'.

Traditional land drains are made of clay, are about 30 cm (1 ft) long, and 10 cm (4 in) wide, though different diameters may be available for use in the main and subsidiary drains. There are plastic alternatives.

Mulching with bulky organic material will help the plants in the short term and the soil in the long term if you work the organic matter into the surface at the end of each season.

Liming will usually help too, but always check the pH first – you will not want to increase the alkalinity if you want to grow acid-loving plants for instance. Lime helps because the calcium that it contains is absorbed strongly by the clay and helps it to form crumbs. Some of its action is indirect: by increasing the alkalinity on an acid clay, earthworms will be encouraged, which in combination with plenty of organic matter will help to improve the structure. It may also improve the availability of some nutrients.

The calcium in gypsum is also absorbed by the clay particles, and has a similar effect to lime, but it does not alter the pH. Its main use, however, is in soil that has been flooded by sea water, as it offsets the effect of the sodium.

Clay cures are often advertised, and are usually based on either lime or gypsum, an organic manure, or inert substances such as expanded clay granules that have a physical effect on the soil. It is unlikely that these will be any more successful than the methods already described. You will also find some so expensive that it could make it cheaper to buy your vegetables, for instance, than to improve the soil sufficiently to grow them.

Planting in Heavy Soil
For vegetable seeds fluid sowing may help (see page 80), or for transplanted vegetables you could improve a small seedbed with sand and peat.

If you are planting trees, shrubs, or herbaceous border plants, it is best to plant in spring rather than autumn. They will then have the summer to become established before having to cope with cold, wet soil. But the plants will have to be watered well in dry weather, and will benefit from a mulch. If planting in autumn, do it early – September is a good time.

Whatever time you plant, take out a bigger hole than usual, and dig in plenty of organic matter (garden compost or peat), also mixing some with the soil to be returned to the planting hole. If using a container-grown plant, tease out a few roots from the rootball, and spread them out. Do not compress the returned soil as firmly as you would normally do.

Besides being heavy and difficult to work, clay soils tend to shrink and crack badly in dry weather. They can be improved by the addition of organic matter.

Digging and Soil Care

For the great majority of plants, even vegetables, regular deep digging is neither necessary nor advisable. In the flower garden, established shrub and herbaceous borders cannot be dug regularly, and beds used for seasonal bedding are often forked over to clear the bed for the next crop as much as to improve fertility.

Why Dig?
In nature plants grow perfectly well without intervention, but both observation and scientific experiments have shown that digging does have beneficial effects, particularly in improving soil structure. Often it is not the digging itself that does the most good, but the

opportunity it gives to incorporate organic material such as bulky manures or garden compost. But even most no-digging systems depend on initial digging to get the soil in good condition to start with.

When to Dig
Early winter is the traditional time to dig a vegetable plot. If the ground is left rough-dug (not raked smooth), a larger surface area will be exposed to winter frosts and to the effects of constant thawing and freezing, moistening and drying. This means that the soil is easier to break down into a fine tilth for sowing or planting in spring.

Heavy soils This is also good advice for heavy soils with a high clay content, and it is a good idea to try to get these dug before late autumn, otherwise the soil may be too wet and sticky, if not frozen, when you want to dig. If it is impossible to dig the whole plot so soon, concentrate on those parts that will form the seedbeds next spring. Try to finish digging by Christmas – do it after that time only if the ground is not waterlogged (otherwise you will damage the soil structure).

If the digging was done during the winter, it will not be necessary to dig again in spring. It should be sufficient to rake the soil level once the soil is dry enough to walk on without sticking to your shoes. Rake in any necessary fertilizers at the same time.

Weeds should be easy to hoe off at this time. Alternatively you can use a contact weedkiller such as paraquat/diquat (if they are mainly annual weeds) or glyphosate (if there are difficult perennial weeds too). Using weedkillers is more practical for a vegetable plot than for a flower border – they can be applied more easily between the rows of plants. In a flower border it may be necessary to paint the weedkiller on individual plants.

Medium soils These also benefit from winter digging, but it is less important.

Light soils These can be dug in spring, leaving just enough time for the soil to settle before you sow or plant. It is usually best to dig a light soil from January onwards, but if dug too soon a surface cap may form as a result of heavy rainfall. This hard soil cap can impede germination. If such a cap does form, break the surface up again by raking and hoeing.

How Deep?
There are digging techniques that penetrate three spits deep (a spit is the depth of a spade blade – about 25 cm/10 in). But this is necessary only in very exceptional circumstances. Most root activity occurs in the top 30–60 cm (1–2 ft) of soil. Even with trees, whose roots may eventually spread deep and wide, it is only necessary to provide a planting hole of about 45 cm (1½ ft) deep.

Double digging (see opposite), in which the soil is cultivated to a depth of two spits deep (about 50 cm/20 in) is worthwhile if drainage is poor, or if a hard pan has formed, perhaps through years of mechanical cultivation to the same depth. A pan is a hard, almost impermeable layer of soil.

An Alternative to Digging

In the ornamental garden comparatively little digging is necessary. Well planted shrub borders with established ground cover will not even need regular forking over, and in the herbaceous border the hoe will be more use than the spade or fork. In both cases, soil structure and fertility will be maintained by regular mulching – and by not walking on the soil when it is wet and likely to be compressed.

It is the vegetable plot that is generally dug routinely, but even here it can easily be reduced to a job to be done say every three, four, or five years.

No-digging systems depend for their success partly on heavy dressings of compost and manures, that are gradually worked into the ground by worms and other soil creatures, and partly by avoiding compaction (which means not walking on the soil more than absolutely necessary, especially when it is wet).

Start digging vacant ground by removing a trench. Barrow the soil to the other end of the plot, or put it to one side to fill in the last trench.

Throw the soil forward from the next row to fill in the trench, inverting each bite of earth to bury any weeds and plant debris.

Single digging If you are digging an open area of ground, such as a vegetable plot, it is best to work methodically to make the digging, and the levelling afterwards, easier.

● Take out a trench the width and depth of a spade blade, and barrow the soil to the other end of the plot.

● If there is a dense covering of perennial weeds, deal with these first by using a weedkiller over the whole area and wait for this to work, or slice them off before digging the next row of soil.

● A spade will enable you to dig cleanly and to an even depth, and is essential if you have to slice through root-matted or grass-covered soil as you dig. For light, sandy soil, or heavy soil relatively free of weeds, you may find a fork will make the work easier. Turn the soil over and invert the clod in the space left where the previous row was moved.

● If using a spade and the soil is heavy or weedy, push the blade into the soil at right angles to the row to mark the position of the next 'bite'. This will enable the next spadeful of soil to be lifted out cleanly.

● Lift the spadeful of soil by bending and then straightening the knees a little, so that they take some of the strain and save the back. Keep the bites small, and lift the spade just high enough to flick the clod forward while inverting it. Taking small bites will be less likely to cause strain and injury, and you will probably do the job more quickly because it will be less tiring.

● When some form of organic matter has to be added, fork or rake it over the trench before the next row is dug. Don't dig it into the second spit, as it will be more beneficial near the surface, where most of the roots are.

Double digging This is worthwhile if the soil is poorly drained or has a hard compacted layer about 30 cm (1 ft) down (although if this is simply due to shallow soil and there is, say, underlying chalk, double digging is not advisable). It may also be worth double digging if you want very good results from crops such as sweet peas or celery that like a deep, rich soil. But all crops can be grown successfully without this additional chore.

It is usual to single dig to the depth of a spit, which is the height of a spade's blade.

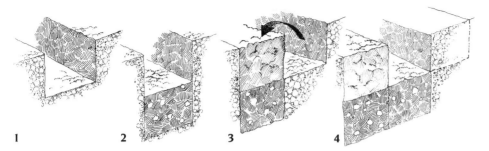

1   2   3   4

Double digging is necessary only if drainage is poor, or if you want to increase the depth of topsoil. It can be useful for some exhibition vegetables, but you can usually grow satisfactory crops without it.

1 *Take out a trench about 60 cm (2 ft) wide and 25 cm (10 in) deep.*

2 *Fork over the bottom of the trench. You can add manure to the bottom spit, but it may do more good in the top 25 cm (10 in).*

3 *Excavate the next trench, throwing the inverted soil forward to fill in the previous trench.*

4 *Fork over the bottom of this trench, and continue until the plot has been dug. Fill in the last trench with soil excavated from the first.*

● Use a garden line to keep the trenches straight. Excavate a trench one spit (about 25 cm/10 in) deep and about 60 cm (2 ft) wide. If you are taking out a single trench for, say, runner beans, simply pile the soil alongside the trench, otherwise barrow it to the other end of the plot to fill in the final trench.

● Spread compost or manure over the bottom of the trench, and then fork this in. Forking the manure into the bottom of the trench will help if you are trying to break up a hard pan or want to improve drainage, but if the compost or manure is mainly for the benefit of the crop, it will probably do more good in the upper layers of the soil – in which case fork the bottom of the trench first, and work the compost or manure into the top spit.

● Excavate the next trench, using the soil to fill in the previous trench.

The Right Tools
Spade This is one garden tool that you really cannot do without. Even if you do not need to do much regular digging you will still need one for planting trees and shrubs, and for other routine jobs.

For lots of heavy digging buy a digging spade (these have a full-sized blade), but if you want one mainly for working amongst border plants or shrubs, or for planting, a border spade (which is smaller) will be lighter to use and adequate for the job.

You will almost certainly find a stainless steel spade the easiest to work with, but they are about three times the cost of most ordinary spades.

The shaft and hilt are likely to be the weak points. Traditionally they were wooden, but don't be put off metal handles (they are usually plastic-covered), they can be as strong as the best wooden ones and stronger than some.

Fork These also have different-sized heads. Digging forks, the most suitable for the majority of garden jobs, usually have heads about 29 cm (11½ in) long and about 20 cm (8 in) wide. Border forks, which are worth considering if you find digging heavy work, or want to work among plants, have a smaller head about 22 cm (8¾ in) deep and 14 cm (5½ in) across. You can occasionally find forks between these sizes.

Stainless steel has less of an advantage for forks than it does for spades. It is usually relatively easy to push a fork through the ground and the soil is not likely to stick to it. A possible solution might be to buy a relatively inexpensive fork but to invest in an expensive, stainless steel spade.

Pros and cons of cultivators A powered cultivator is worth buying only if you have a large area of ground that needs regular cultivation. For the occasional job, or when constructing a new garden, it will be cheaper to hire one.

● A cultivator will not be as efficient as a spade for burying weeds, and it will actually increase those easily multiplied by division – such as couch grass. This can be overcome by very frequent cultivation or by using a suitable weed-killer (see page 134).

● If you want to buy a cultivator, one with an electric engine is likely to cost less than a petrol cultivator, and it will be quieter and cleaner to use. But the trailing flex and the problem of a convenient power supply are severe limitations.

- Petrol-powered cultivators are generally more powerful and more versatile, but they are noisy and heavy to use, and there are fumes too.

- Rear-engined cultivators have the rotors on a pole-like boom. This makes them easy to manoeuvre and they are used by sweeping the boom from side to side as you work forwards. It is also easier to dig a hole with this type, and they are easy to handle between rows.

- Front-engined cultivators have wheels below the engine, with the rotors behind the wheels. Because of this arrangement the wheels are powered and despite their usually large size they are not very tiring to use.

- Mid-engined cultivators have the rotors beneath the engine, and the weight of the engine helps them to dig into the ground. The rotors both cultivate the ground and pull the machine along, which can make them quite difficult to control.

This picture shows plants thriving in a dry border. If resources are limited it may be better to grow tolerant plants than to try to change the nature of the soil.

Manures and Fertilizers

The words 'fertilizer' and 'manure' are often used synonymously. Both are substances applied to the soil to make it more fruitful but manure is more correctly used for a bulky humus-forming material that is of vegetable or animal origin. It is applied in large quantity, its main purpose being to improve the soil structure. Fertilizers provide plants with nutrients to improve growth and quality. They are applied in small quantities and are of two main types: inorganic or organic.

Manures
Manures are very low in nutrients, especially as they usually have to be stacked and left to mature before it is safe to use them close to plants. Their value lies in the contribution they make to improving soil structure – the humus that they ultimately provide after action by soil organisms will make the best of what nutrients are available, and the improved water-retention or drainage (depending on the problem with the soil originally), and generally improved soil conditions will contribute much to plant health far beyond their nutrient value. Other, non-animal, products have much the same effect: peat, spent hops, and garden compost will all have a beneficial effect on soil structure even though they are lower in nutrients.

Animal manures are always worth having if you can obtain them. The nutrient value of all animal manure can vary widely and it will also be affected by how it has been stored. Do not dig in fresh manure otherwise there may be a temporary loss of fertility owing to the heavy demands of the soil organisms on the available nitrogen. In practical terms it is best to ignore the nutrients and regard them simply as bonus. Bulky animal manures are well worth using to benefit soil structure alone.

Peat will improve moisture-retention and soil structure, but its contribution to the nutrient reserves of the soil will be minimal, and as it is expensive in comparison with most of the alternatives it is probably best reserved for localized use when planting, or for mulching (see page 31). Other soil improvers such as vermiculite and perlite fall into this category.

Green manuring involves growing a leafy crop such as mustard, rape, vetches, lupins, even rye grass, which is dug into the soil when it is about 25 cm (10 in) high. It is unlikely that green manuring will do much to improve soil structure but if timed properly it may help to make nutrients that might otherwise be lost available to the following crop – the green manure crop can use and store nitrogen, for instance, releasing it again during decomposition. But to make use of this you need to plant soon after the green manure has been dug in.

How much to apply Unlike fertilizers, the manures are difficult to over-do provided they are not too 'fresh'. As a guide, however, you need to apply at least 5.4 kg per sq m (10 lb per sq yd) *every year* to maintain a high level of organic matter in the soil.

Unless you are fortunate enough to have a plentiful local supply of inexpensive bulky manures it is unlikely that you will be able to obtain enough of any one of the manures mentioned, and you will probably have to use a combination of them.

See also mulching, page 31.

Artificial or Natural?
The so-called artificial fertilizers are simple salts such as ammonium sulphate (sulphate of ammonia) and potassium sulphate (sulphate of potash). When dissolved in the soil water, these break down to a form easily assimilated directly by the plants. But when manure is added to the soil, it has to be worked on by micro-organisms to break it down into simpler elements before the nutrients become available. There is often controversy over which is best: synthetic fertilizers or natural organic manures, but it is important to remember that the nutrients taken up by the plants are identical, regardless of the original source.

Fertilizers
Fertilizers add no bulk to the soil, and contribute nothing to the soil structure. They simply provide the basic nutrients. Some of them are 'organic' like bonemeal and hoof and horn, others are 'synthetic' or man-made like superphosphate and sulphate of ammonia.

'Straight' fertilizers are those manufactured fertilizers like sulphate of potash or superphosphate, for which the manufacturer can make no special claims as they are standard products. Compound or balanced fertilizers contain a mixture of several fertilizers in various proportions – sometimes balanced for one particular type of crop (say roses, chrysanthemums or lawns), sometimes they are intended as general-purpose fertilizers likely to benefit most crops.

Concentrated organic fertilizers In the past this heading might have included things like soot and dissolved bones. Nowadays there are relatively few everyday fertilizers in this category, and most of them are by-products of the abattoir. See table opposite.

Concentrated artificial fertilizers These are generally a less expensive way to apply the basic plant nutrients than using concentrated organic fertilizers. They are usually quicker-acting.

NITROGENOUS FERTILIZERS
Nitrate of soda contains nitrogen in a form which is soluble in water and is assimilated by the plant at once. For that reason it is of most use for giving plants such as spring cabbages a boost of growth in spring. A common analysis is 15.5% nitrogen, and it should be applied as a topdressing only to crops needing a quick boost, at about 35 g/sq m (1 oz/sq yd), hoed in.

Sulphate of ammonia contains nitrogen in the form of an ammonium salt which has to be converted to nitrate by soil bacteria before it can be absorbed by

Fertilizer Labels

Most fertilizers contain one or more of the major nutrients nitrogen (N), phosphorus (P), and potassium (K), and in Britain the amount of each element must be shown on the bag. A shorthand method is used to show how much of each is contained in a compound fertilizer, known as the N:P:K ratio. The bag illustrated contains 5% nitrogen (N), 10% phosphorus (P_2O_5) and 10% potassium (K_2O). There may also be trace-elements present and these will be indicated by the percentage against their chemical symbol.

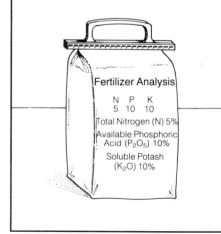

Fertilizer Analysis

N P K
5 10 10

Total Nitrogen (N) 5%
Available Phosphoric Acid (P_2O_5) 10%
Soluble Potash (K_2O) 10%

Organic Fertilizers

Fertilizer and main nutrient	Properties	When and how much to use
Hoof and horn meal Nitrogen 12–14% N	Acts fairly quickly in warm moist soils and is long lasting. The finer it is ground the more quickly the fertilizer becomes available	Ground preparation. 150–200 g/sq m (4–6 oz/sq yd)
Dried Blood Nitrogen 12–14% N	Quick acting but expensive.	Used as topdressing for actively growing plants. 75–100 g/sq m (2–3 oz/sq yd)
Blood, Meat and Bone Meal (or blood, fish and bone) Nitrogen and Phosphates 3% N, 9% P_2O_5 5% K	Good for general use. The nitrogen acts quickly but the phosphates are only slowly available.	Sprinkle on soil and rake in in spring. 150 g/sq m (4 oz/sq yd)
Bonemeal Phosphates and Nitrogen 21% P_2O_5 4% N	Slow-acting phosphatic fertilizer. Has a useful nitrogen content which works quickly.	Use in flower borders in autumn or spring, especially when planting. 200 g/sq m (6 oz/sq yd)
Wood Ashes Potash 2–6% K	Freshly made ash from young plant material is best. Do not give large dressings to alkaline soils because ash makes the problem worse.	Apply in autumn or winter ahead of sowing or planting. 200 g/sq m (6 oz/sq yd)

the plant, and it is therefore slower-acting than the previous fertilizer. This can be a benefit if it is used as a base dressing and worked into the soil in spring, for instance, before sowing or planting. Its normal analysis is 20.6% nitrogen.

Sulphate of ammonia reacts with the soil, leading to a loss of an equivalent amount of lime. So for 50 g of sulphate of ammonia applied, approximately 50 g of lime will be lost. If your soil is too alkaline this may be beneficial, but you may not want to use it on already acid soils.

Nitro-chalk is a proprietary compound consisting of chalk and ammonium nitrate. Half the nitrogen is present as ammonia, the other half as nitrate, and the usual analysis is 15.5% nitrogen, 48% carbonate of lime (chalk). It is not normally used as a base dressing, but as a booster. It is usually used at about 35 g/sq m (1 oz/sq yd).

Where the ground is naturally wet and boggy, it's best to leave it and to grow moisture-loving plants.

Terms Explained

Compound fertilizers are those that contain two or more nutrients.

Foliar feeds are liquid fertilizers (or powders that can be made into a solution), often containing trace elements as well as the major nutrients. They are easily absorbed by the leaves and quick acting.

Slow-release fertilizers are mainly used in potting composts or to apply to plants growing in pots – the nutrients are released slowly over a long period. Controlled release fertilizers release their nutrients only when the temperature is warm enough for growth – reducing the risk of over-stimulating the plant when the weather is too cold.

Straight fertilizers supply only one of the major nutrients (nitrogen *or* potassium for example).

Trace elements are nutrients required in very small amounts and are not normally applied (except in some liquid feeds) routinely. *Fritted trace elements* are bonded to fine glass particles (frits) and are released slowly over a long period.

If you have a neutral soil you will be able to grow most plants well, but even if you have one of the more extreme soils, the range of plants that will grow well will still be vast. The garden above contains acid-loving plants, the one on the left is planted with lime-loving plants such as dianthus and campanulas.

PHOSPHATIC FERTILIZERS

Superphosphate of lime (superphosphate) has a name that can lead to confusion. The lime that it contains is in a form valueless to plants, a fact that should be reassuring if you want to use it on plants that are lime-haters. The soluble phosphate dissolves in soil water to form phosphoric acid – the form in which it is absorbed by plants. A typical analysis is 18% phosphoric acid (P_2O_5). Although fast-acting, it does not suffer from the drawback of a rapid loss of nutrients from the soil, as phosphates are better held by the soil and are less likely to be leached. For that reason one application before sowing or planting is likely to be adequate for the year. A typical rate of application is 150 g/sq m (4 oz/sq yd). It can be used as a topdressing at the same rate.

Basic slag, a by-product of steel manufacture, is seldom used nowadays. It has a phosphoric acid content of about 14%, and also contains a little lime. Because it is slower-acting than superphosphate it is usually applied in late autumn for the next year's crop. Quality and analysis can vary, but it is usually applied at about 150 g/sq m (4 oz/sq yd).

POTASH FERTILIZERS

Sulphate of potash is the purest form of potash you are likely to buy, and a typical analysis is 48.5%. It can be applied at the beginning of the season, but is also useful during the season as a supplement for crops likely to benefit from extra potash. Application rates usually vary from 35–150 g/sq m (1–4 oz/sq yd).

Muriate of potash contains more potash than sulphate of potash (usually 60.6%), but it is less pure and there may be chlorides present that are toxic to the roots of young plants – the danger is greatest in dry soils. It is usually used at 35–75 g/sq m (1–2 oz/sq yd) a month before the seeds are sown so that any harmful impurities have a chance to be washed out of the soil. It stores badly.

OTHER FERTILIZERS

The fertilizers below are used to treat some of the most frequently found minor and trace element deficiencies; they will not often be needed.

Sulphate of magnesium (magnesium sulphate) is better known as Epsom salt. It is usually applied at about 35 g/sq m (1 oz/sq yd), but should only be used when there is a magnesium deficiency (see page 68).

Sulphate of manganese (manganese sulphate) is mixed with water (6 g in 5 litres/1 oz in 5 gallons) and sprayed on plants suffering from manganese deficiency (see page 68).

Sulphate of iron (ferrous sulphate) is best diluted in the same way as manganese sulphate and sprayed on if iron deficiency has been diagnosed (see page 68). It may be easier, if lime-induced iron chlorosis is the problem, to use a chelated iron (Sequestrene). Both manganese and iron are likely to be locked up and unavailable to plants in a very alkaline soil, and both these elements can be supplied in the one Sequestrene treatment.

Borax is likely to be necessary on a very few soils, and only where boron-deficiency disorders such as brown heart in turnips are a known problem. Spray vulnerable plants with a borax solution of 6 g to 1 litre (1 oz to 1 gallon) of water.

Mulching

A mulch has three main functions:
● It conserves soil moisture
● It helps to control weeds
● It eventually improves soil structure

As a bonus:
● Some mulches can improve the appearance of the bed
● Some can protect low-growing crops – such as strawberries – from mud splashes in heavy rain
● They can reduce soil temperature variations

If Resources are Limited

If you have only a limited amount of suitable mulching material and don't want to buy any, use what you have got wisely. Instead of spreading a very thin layer over a wide area, concentrate it deeply in a small area round those plants that will benefit most.

Give priority to newly-planted trees and shrubs, to soft fruit such as raspberries, and to those crops that will benefit most from water conservation.

Using a mulch

Always make the mulch deep enough to be effective. Bulky organic mulches should be at least 5 cm (2 in) deep. Do not expect plastic, stone or gravel mulches to do much to improve the soil – they are primarily used to control weeds and conserve moisture.

Make sure that the soil structure is reasonable before you mulch (it

should not be compacted), and apply the mulch for a radius of about 60 cm (2 ft) around a shrub or young tree. If mulching vegetables, make sure it extends 30 cm (1 ft) either side of the row. A herbaceous border can be

blanket mulched, provided the material is kept off the actual plant stems. Never let the mulch touch the stems, otherwise they may rot, and in the case of grafted shrubs the grafted section may root.

A mulch acts as a barrier, reducing water loss from the soil by evaporation. And if thick enough (or impenetrable enough – a polythene sheet is thin but still a good barrier), it will prevent the germination and establishment of most weed seedlings. Organic mulches will also rot down and provide humus which will help to provide a reservoir of nutrients.

The use of mulches for conserving water is described on page 48, and for weed control on page 135.

Mulches of organic material are also very useful soil conditioners. Rotted manure, garden compost, straw, peat, and sawdust for example, will all gradually be incorporated into the soil in time. And in doing so most of them will provide nutrients, or the humus formed will help the soil to retain nutrients, improving both structure and nutrient

balance. They will also help indirectly by encouraging more worms – which will in turn improve the soil – and directly by preventing soil capping (the formation of a hard surface crust).

Most organic mulches, such as manure or garden compost are acid, and this can be useful if you are trying to lower the pH. If your soil is already too acid, try mulching with spent mushroom compost, which should be alkaline. Or use a polythene mulch.

Some organic mulches, such as well-rotted manure or garden compost, straw, sawdust, and pulverized bark, take nitrogen from the soil as they break down. To overcome this it may be worth applying a nitrogenous fertilizer at about 35 g/sq m (1 oz/sq yd) before the mulch is laid.

Because it will be difficult to apply dry fertilizers once the mulch is in position, it is best to use these before the mulch. Always mulch on damp soil.

A mulch applied in spring should last through to autumn, when it can be forked in. Be careful not to disturb shallow-rooting plants when doing this.

Making Garden Compost

A compost heap is often regarded as something smelly, untidy, and not quite nice. It can be all those things if you simply throw your kitchen and garden waste onto an unstructured heap. Properly made, however, a compost heap will recycle most kitchen and garden waste, without any of those drawbacks. It is almost impossible to have too much compost, so it is worth acquiring the knack of making good compost.

To work efficiently, a compost heap has to be large enough to heat up sufficiently to destroy weed seeds and diseased material. The right condition must be provided for the aerobic bacteria (those which need oxygen) and fungi responsible for quick decomposition to thrive. That means you should 'turn' the heap a couple of times to let more air into it and to bring the outer layers of unrotted material to the centre. You do not *have* to do this; anaerobic bacteria (not needing oxygen) will take over but they work more slowly.

Size is most important – a single heap should be at least 1 cu m (35 cu ft). If you make it smaller than this it probably will not heat up enough to make good compost quickly.

You can add most soft kitchen vegetable refuse such as peelings as well as egg shells, and all except very woody garden refuse can go on it too, though it is best to burn diseased material.

Lawn mowings will rot down well but it is best to intersperse them with layers of other materials. Hedge and shrub prunings, and autumn leaves, will probably benefit from a compost activator (which you can buy), or by balancing these with a nitrogen-rich material such as animal manure. Sulphate of ammonia should work out cheaper than a compost activator and will probably be as successful. Sawdust, newspapers, and cardboard will also rot down if an activator or some other source of nitrogen is provided.

Try to add a 23 cm (9 in) layer each time, as this will help the bacterial activity. You can store the waste in a polythene bag until you have enough.

If you do not use a proper bin, good compost can be made in a free-standing heap if it is large enough. Build it up in layers, with coarse material at the base and sides sloping slightly inwards towards the top. Keep it moist but not wet (cover it with a sheet of polythene weighted down with bricks). Once the heap has reached the required height and heated up, turn it after about 10 days, rebuilding it again.

Proprietary compost bins may look more attractive but they are unlikely to be any better at making compost than a home-made heap.

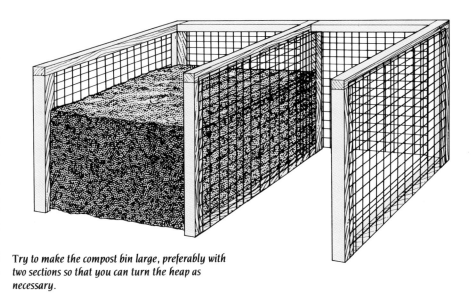

Try to make the compost bin large, preferably with two sections so that you can turn the heap as necessary.

The Climate

Climate will affect your plants almost as much as the soil. No matter how suitable the ground, if the site is too cold or too windy, or even too hot and dry, there will be some plants that will not grow successfully unless protected in some way.

Climatic Limitations

The weather changes not only from day to day, but sometimes from minute to minute. If interpreted as the combination of temperature, sunlight, rainfall, and wind strength, for instance, it will even vary at any one time *within* the garden. *Climate* is in effect the mixture of the weather patterns for the area, and there are well-known regional climatic variations within the British Isles. But basing assumptions of climate for a particular year on past records has its limitations. In some summers, areas of normally low rainfall (such as East Anglia) may have more rain than normally wetter areas, and while the South West is known for its mild winters, in some years it can have more snow than many of the traditionally 'cold' regions. Figures and dates based on past records are useful but can be no guarantee of the coming season. For example, occasionally there will be an abnormally late frost when some plants may be lost. With gardening you have to take some risks.

Sunlight

Sunlight is an essential element for healthy growth of all green plants, it also often determines at what time of year a plant flowers.

Despite its tropical appearance, this yucca is perfectly hardy in Britain. Unfortunately many shrubs are more vulnerable and losses may follow a hard winter.

The sun provides light and is a source of warmth and energy too. The earth loses heat to outer space constantly in the form of long-wave radiation, but fortunately short-wave radiation from the sun makes good the losses. It is the ability of glass to allow short-wave radiation to pass easily while hindering long-wave radiation that creates the greenhouse effect (see page 51).

Sunlight not only warms the air, which usually speeds up biological processes, it also supplies the energy for photosynthesis.

Light requirements of plants vary, although no green self-supporting plant can live in complete darkness. The gardener can arrive at a rough assessment of a plant's need for light by noting the colour of the leaf and whether it is thick or thin. For example, a plant with thick dark green leaves is in all probability a shade plant, whereas one with thin, light green leaves (or variegated leaves which lack chlorophyll) needs all possible light.

Shade plants In a permanently shady part of the garden it is best to grow only those plants naturally adapted to low light levels. Their leaves contain more chlorophyll than those of sun-lovers, which makes them more efficient in producing sugars. But with less light available they are unlikely to produce as much sugar as plants in sun, and are generally slow-growing.

Other effects of light Sunlight is important for photosynthesis (page 55) and

Day Length

The ratio between the length of day and night determines the flowering time of many plants, which is why in the garden some plants will flower only at certain times of the year. For example, a plant such as chrysanthemum grows when days are long and nights are short (summer) and flowers when the days shorten and nights lengthen. The internal clock that tells a plant when to grow or flower is influenced by a chemical called phytochrome that is sensitive to light.

Commercial growers use this fact to advantage and by artificially adjusting day length by the use of black-out material or lights at appropriate times, they can bring plants into flower at 'unnatural' times of year. This technique is widely used in nurseries for the production of all-the-year-round chrysanthemums, as well as the more seasonal crops of poinsettia and kalanchoe. Chrysanthemum and other plants exhibiting the same characteristics are known as short day plants. Those plants which grow when days are short and nights long but flower when days are long and nights short are called long day plants. Some plants flower regardless of the length of day, and the temperature is also an important factor.

therefore growth, but it has other profound effects on plants. Plants that are grown in shade are often spindly and pale, and many will 'turn' towards the light. This is because sunlight destroys one group of plant hormones known as auxins that cause the plant to elongate. If it is not arrested by light the auxin will cause the stem to grow upwards abnormally fast – nature's way of encouraging it to reach light. If there is good light coming from one direction the auxin will move to the shady side, and that side will grow faster than the sunny side, so the plant grows towards the light.

When we force rhubarb or blanch celery and chicory and leeks, we turn the plant's response to poor light to our advantage.

Temperature

Temperature can be critical for the germination of flowers and weeds alike, and each plant will also have an optimum temperature for its subsequent growth. For many plants, very high temperatures can be equally as harmful as very low temperatures. For example, a tomato is a subtropical plant which will grow best at around 18°C (65°F). Above this temperature the growth rate slows down and below 5°C (42°F) growth ceases.

The way the germination of seeds can be affected by soil temperature is described on page 44.

Most seeds will simply lie dormant if it is too cold, plants, on the other hand,

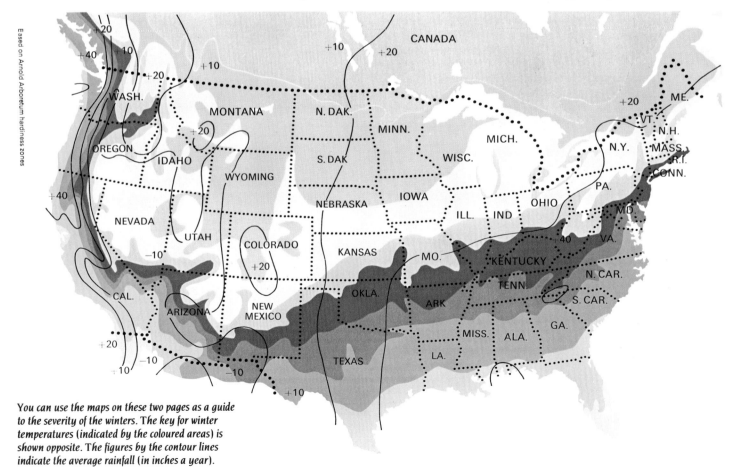

You can use the maps on these two pages as a guide to the severity of the winters. The key for winter temperatures (indicated by the coloured areas) is shown opposite. The figures by the contour lines indicate the average rainfall (in inches a year).

may be damaged or killed. For the majority of plants grown, cold temperatures merely slow down growth and put the plant into a form of hibernation, but 'tender' plants are those that are likely to be killed if the temperature drops to freezing or below.

Truly tender (or half-hardy) plants, such as fibrous-rooted begonias and coleus, will be completely killed by even a slight frost; the top growth of plants such as dahlias and fuchsias will be killed but unless the frost is severe the rootstock (roots and stems below ground level) will survive. Other plants succumb only as the temperature be-

The shaded areas relate to the severity of the winter. In the United States, where the climate can be more extreme than in Britain, hardiness zones are often given to indicate if a plant is likely to survive in a particular area. The zones represent the average annual minimum temperature in degrees F.

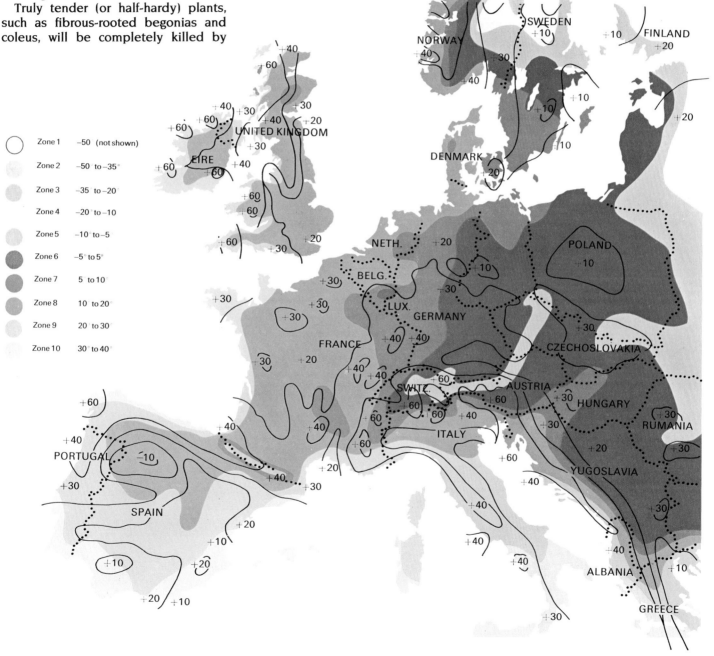

Zone 1	−50 (not shown)
Zone 2	−50° to −35°
Zone 3	−35° to −20°
Zone 4	−20° to −10°
Zone 5	−10° to −5°
Zone 6	−5° to 5°
Zone 7	5° to 10°
Zone 8	10° to 20°
Zone 9	20° to 30°
Zone 10	30° to 40°

comes steadily colder or the freeze more prolonged. A light frost may not kill theoretically tender plants such as pelargoniums and the creeping fig (*Ficus pumila*), but a long or severe frost certainly will. Sweet bay trees (*Laurus nobilis*) may survive for 20 or so winters in some areas without damage, only to be killed by an abnormally cold spell.

Susceptibility to frost also varies according to the stage of growth. New growth is more tender than old growth and growth that is full of moisture is more susceptible than that which is not. This is one reason for keeping greenhouse and house plants on the dry side in winter if they are growing in poorly heated surroundings.

Snow is less of a problem than frost: a thick covering will provide insulation for the plants underneath.

Wind

Wind can cause direct damage (flowers may be beaten to the ground; even trees get blown down), but it has less obvious effects too.

● In extremely exposed sites, the wind actually achieves a form of natural pruning, and this can often be seen in trees shaped by the wind in coastal areas.

● It also has a profound effect on temperature, and therefore growth. The air currents keep the surface temperature lower than they would be in still air (although on a cold cloudless night they may actually help to prevent ground frost).

● Because strong winds can lower the soil temperature by about 2°C, it means

Plants For a Windy Site

If you have a garden exposed to winds, there may be problems even if there is a shelter-belt, in which case it is best to concentrate on establishing a framework of shrubs and trees that will stand the harsh conditions and provide some shelter for other less robust plants.

RECOMMENDED SHRUBS
Arundinaria japonica
Calluna spp
*Cotoneaster horizontalis, C. simonsii**
Elaeagnus pungens 'Maculata'*
Erica spp
*Escallonia***
*Griselinia litoralis***
Helianthemum
*Hippophae rhamnoides**
Hydrangea macrophylla
*Olearia macrodonta***
*Pittosporum tenuifolium***

RECOMMENDED TREES
Acer pseudoplatanus
Alnus cordata
Crataegus monogyna
× *Cupressocyparis leylandii*
Cupressus macrocarpa
Fraxinus excelsior
Laurus nobilis
Pinus sylvestris
Prunus nigra, P. cerasifera
Quercus ilex
Sorbus aria, S. *aucuparia*

Spartium junceum
Tamarix gallica, T. *tetrandra*
Ulex europaeus

* = Can also be used as a hedge or shelter-belt.
** = Not dependably hardy in all areas, but suitable for windy coastal sites except in very cold districts.

Olearia macrodonta

Elaeagnus pungens 'Maculata'

A wind-pruned tree, highlighting a strong prevailing wind in this area. Buds on the windward side of the tree have been dehydrated and damaged more than those on the leeward side, which led to this uneven growth. Prevailing winds strong enough to cause this kind of damage are most likely in coastal areas or in exposed open areas without windbreaks.

that germination temperatures may not occur until later in spring, and germination and early growth may also be affected by the rapid drying out of the surface soil.

● The cooling effect of the wind has a considerable influence on heat loss from the greenhouse and for this reason siting the greenhouse in a sheltered position is likely to save on heating costs.

● Wind can affect plants by increasing the rate at which water is lost from the leaves by evaporation and this can profoundly influence a newly-planted shrub in leaf which will lose water more rapidly in a windy position and, as the roots will probably be unable to take up water fast enough to replace that lost, it may die or suffer damage from which it is slow to recover. Planting dormant plants with no leaves overcomes this problem. But with evergreens there will always be some leaves and, for this reason, those planted in an exposed position should be given wind protection until established. An anti-desiccant spray will also help.

● Wind damage may cause leaf scorching on plants other than those newly planted. Symptoms show as browning of the leaf edges or a mottled browning of the whole leaf. It is difficult to distinguish these symptoms from those of frost damage and a little detective work may be necessary to determine the cause.

● Newly planted trees and shrubs can also suffer from wind rock, which weakens the root hold in the soil and prevents the formation of the small fibrous roots.

Humidity

This can be defined as the amount of moisture in the atmosphere. It is something you are seldom aware of until you go into a well-maintained warm greenhouse, yet it is crucially important to plants.

Humidity affects the plant directly by influencing the rate of transpiration (more water is transpired if the air is dry, and it stops if the air is saturated), and indirectly by affecting the rate of evaporation from the soil.

The level of humidity also influences the growth and spread of many diseases: fungus disease spores germinate rapidly in a humid atmosphere, and the diseases can grow more rapidly than in dry, moving air.

Low humidity, especially in high temperatures, puts stress on many plants, unless they are naturally adapted for arid conditions, such as the cacti and other succulents. The amount of moisture held by the air varies with the temperature – hot air can contain more water than cold air and many plants requiring high temperatures also need high levels of humidity. This is the reason why controlling or increasing the humidity is an important factor in greenhouse management and also in growing houseplants successfully.

Rainfall

There are regional rainfall patterns that mean some parts of the country are naturally drier than others. Apart from influencing the amount of watering required, this will also affect the types of plant that will grow best.

Hills and valleys

Altitude can have a more profound effect on plant growth than is often appreciated. Valleys are generally warmer and sheltered, the hills more exposed to wind and cold. As the ground height increases the average air and soil temperatures decrease, rainfall and wind are likely to increase. The effect of this can be to shorten the growing season of most plants at higher levels.

Even if you live in a valley, the weather may depend on which side of the hill range you garden. On the leeward side the air warms up, dispersing the clouds, often giving sunnier, warmer, and drier weather. On the windward side the rising moist air cools giving more clouds and rain.

Unfortunately valleys have their problems too, and on a calm, cloudless night the surface cools quickly with the warm air rising and the cold air slipping downwards into the valley, where the night temperatures are likely to be much lower than those on the hillside.

If you garden at a high altitude there will be many plants that simply will not grow well, if at all, and even in simply hilly countryside, the plants in the upland regions will probably be smaller than those growing in the valleys.

Aspect

The orientation of the house and garden will have a great influence on the plants grown. South-facing gardens are warmer and sunnier than north-facing gardens, and on a south-facing slope spring may arrive about 10 days earlier.

Town and country

In the days of heavy atmospheric pollution, some plants were difficult to grow well in towns. Nowadays the cleaner air means that plants are unlikely to be damaged by pollution, and the blanket of warmth created by a city, with its

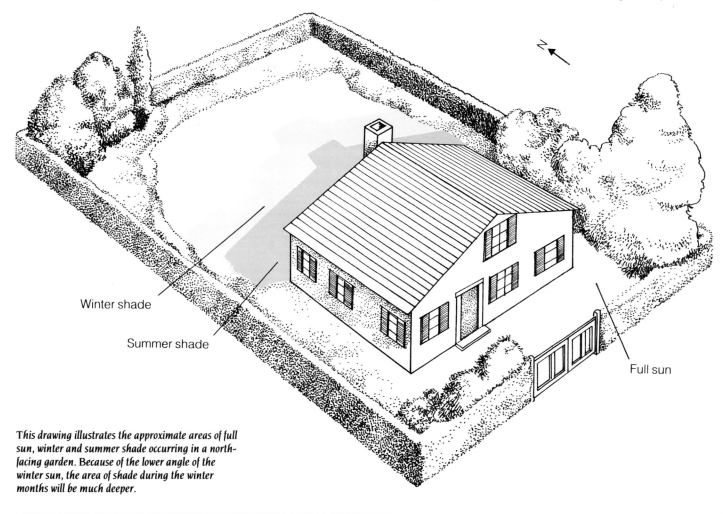

Winter shade

Summer shade

Full sun

This drawing illustrates the approximate areas of full sun, winter and summer shade occurring in a north-facing garden. Because of the lower angle of the winter sun, the area of shade during the winter months will be much deeper.

shelter from buildings and heat generated by city life, will be a positive advantage for many plants that are on the borderline of hardiness. There is an effect known as the heat island phenomenon, where roads and buildings take up heat generated during the day, by people and traffic as well as the sun, and release it during the night. To some extent this reduces the level to which the temperature would otherwise fall – a sort of night-storage heater in reverse.

In inner city areas it is possible to find plants thriving after a hard winter that would probably have been killed in an exposed country garden.

The Microclimate

Most of the climatic effects described so far affect a whole area or region, but there will be local variations even within a small garden or around individual plants and this is known as a microclimate. There will probably be less soil moisture in the lee of buildings, while the space between close neighbouring houses may generate a wind tunnel similar to the effect of coastal winds. The south side of a wall will be warmer than the north side, and will receive more sun. Trees will affect the ground and garden near them. If there are hedges and slopes, some parts will be more sheltered from wind damage but possibly more vulnerable to severe frost.

Do not overlook the effect buildings, hedges and fences have on the amount of rainfall the soil receives. Plants on the sheltered side of these will have to be able to tolerate drier conditions (or be watered more often). Trees and large shrubs will affect the soil around and under them in the same way.

What To Do About It

There are obvious limits to the extent to which you can modify the environment, but there are some positive steps that can be taken. If you live in an exposed position, a hedge or windbreak will make a tremendous difference to the range and quality of the plants that you can grow. The effect of hedges and screens is discussed later, on pages 90 to 95, but if you do not want the work associated with a hedge, there are semi-permeable and non-solid alternatives. A trellis might be more effective than a fence; pierced screen block walling more effective than a solid brick or stone wall.

Where appearance is less important, perhaps around a vegetable garden, one of the artificial windbreaks could be useful. The types usually available are knitted polyethylene (similar to greenhouse shading), moulded polyethylene, and polyethylene and nylon webbing. Most of these should have a life of at least five years, and may go on for ten, and although they do not look elegant they are practical. Most are designed to let through about 50 per cent of the wind. They will not, of course, provide privacy, and the supporting posts will have to be well secured into the ground.

There are areas of a garden that have their own microclimate. Many plants thriving in this sheltered and shaded, moist spot would probably not do well in a more open and exposed position. If a plant doesn't do well in one part, it may be worth moving it.

Avoiding Frost Pockets

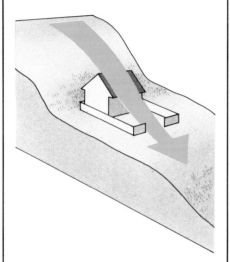

If your garden is on a slope, make sure that hedges and fences do not trap the air in a frost pocket. The emphasis must be on a high, dense hedge at the highest point to reduce the impact of the cold air flowing downwards. The lower boundary should be relatively open to allow cold air to drain away down the hill.

Winter Problems

Shelter-belts and hedges will do much to provide warmer and less windy conditions in the garden, but there will still be the need for extra protection in some parts, or for particularly vulnerable plants. In the shrub border, the more tender or easily wind-damaged plants can be protected by tougher and perhaps taller shrubs nearby. Planting against a protected wall will enable many shrubs on the borderline of hardiness to be grown that would probably fail in a more open aspect.

Avoiding Frost Damage

In almost all parts of the British Isles, there are inevitably frosts and spells of prolonged freezing weather. The majority of plants need no special protection, but if you are trying to grow a plant on the borderline of hardiness, it is worth giving it some extra protection. Even some hardy shrubs may benefit from protection for the first winter if newly planted.

Winter Protection

Some form of protection can mean the difference between life and death for some plants.

● Alpines, especially those with hairy leaves, suffer more from excess moisture in the winter than from the cold. Protect them with a sheet of glass supported on wires or pieces of wood. A cloche could be used, but this is often difficult to position on a rock garden.

● Newly-planted conifers and evergreens may become dehydrated from wind and suffer from windburn. Use a transplanting antidesiccant spray (this puts a short-term coating on the leaves to cut down water loss), or erect a screen of hessian, plastic mesh netting, or polythene around them. Alternatively use wire-reinforced polythene to form a sleeve round the plants, secured to a stake. Whatever material is used, always leave the top open but cover this with polythene on very cold nights.

● A cold frame can be protected with layers of hessian or a piece of old carpet (cover these with a sheet of polythene to keep them dry). Roll it over the frame on very cold nights, but remove it during the day if there are growing plants inside that need light.

● Protect the crowns of half-hardy or slightly tender perennials, especially if you live in a cold district. Put down slug pellets first, then apply a thick layer of straw, bracken, pulverized bark, or even dry peat. It may be worth covering the dry mulch with a sheet of polythene pegged down.

Planting vulnerable plants deeper than normal might also save them in most years unless you live in a very cold area. Fuchsias, gladioli, and dahlias can sometimes be overwintered in the ground with little or no extra protection if planted deeply enough.

● Shrubs in tubs are especially vulnerable because the whole rootball can become frozen. Terracotta tubs may split if water seeps into fine cracks and then freezes. Wrap the container in hessian, and then polythene.

● Wall-trained shrubs that are not dependably hardy in your area are best covered with a sheet of polythene or very fine plastic mesh. In a very cold garden, it may even be worth packing straw or bracken around the branches. Bushy twigs or branches of evergreens pushed into the soil around the plant will also provide some protection.

Other Winter Precautions

Snow is only a problem if it is so heavy that there is a risk of a branch being broken or damaged by it – large conifers and hedges are especially vulnerable and can be damaged if the snow is not shaken or knocked off. Plants beneath the snow are usually perfectly safe, as the snow forms a kind of insulation from the more extreme weather conditions.

Avoid throwing snow from the paths on to the lawn – the turf will begin to suffer if it is covered too long with heavy or compacted snow and ice.

Although the snow will form an insulating blanket over frames and cold or cool greenhouses (it will be melted on a heated and poorly insulated greenhouse), it will cut down light. For that reason it is best to remove the snow with a brush.

Protecting the pond

A thin sheet of ice that lasts for a few days will not harm the pond and its inhabitants. Even thick ice should not cause concern unless the pond is very shallow and the fish do not have a deep area into which they can retreat. The risk to fish comes mainly from the build-up of toxic gases if the pond has been frozen over for a long time – and this can happen whether the ice is 5 cm or 30 cm (2 or 12 in) thick. The surface is the pond's lung, through which indirectly the fish must breathe. For that reason it is important to keep a small area ice-free if possible. The idea of floating balls or other compressible containers on the water is often recommended – but if the weather is

really severe, the water just freezes beneath them and pushes them upwards. They will not keep the water open. The most efficient method is to use an electric pond heater. There are low-voltage heaters available, which are not expensive to run as they simply keep a small area open around the heater itself.

Do not break the ice by pressure. It will stress the fish, and if the pond has been made with a liner, you may tear the liner where the ice has become stuck to it. You can use kettles or pans of water to open up a frozen pond, but you will have to keep replenishing the hot water if the ice is thick, and of course the water may soon freeze over again.

For many alpines, it's not the winter cold that threatens them but too much moisture. A sheet of glass or plastic over the top will prevent choice and vulnerable alpines from becoming too wet around the crown during the winter.

Spring Problems

Late spring frosts are a hazard in any garden. Plants that would come to no harm when dormant may be injured once soft new spring growth has developed. And early blossom may be damaged – blemishing ornamental plants and affecting the set of fruits. Tender plants put out too soon may be killed. It is often possible to give the plants some temporary protection, but unfortunately predicting frost can be difficult. The weather forecast should always alert you, but much depends on your particular locality. Frost is likely in late spring if the wind is from the north or east, the soil dry, and the sky clear of clouds.

The further the air has to travel over land, the lower the dawn temperature is likely to be, which is why inland areas are often more vulnerable to severe or late frosts than coastal areas.

Soil Temperature

The calendar is a useful *guide* to gardening activities, but nothing more. Each season is different, and of course conditions vary not only nationally but locally too.

Spring is the time of most activity, and there is an understandable urge to get seeds planted as soon as possible. The seed packet will give you a useful indication of approximate sowing times, but if the season is late and you sow too early the seeds will not germinate; they will be vulnerable to diseases and may rot, or even be eaten, before they have a chance to germinate. Sowing too early may also mean that although the seeds germinate the seedlings receive a check to growth and grow slowly.

The best guide to sowing is soil temperature. This is easily taken with a soil thermometer (these are inexpensive and can usually be bought from a

The leaves of this Choisya ternata *have been burnt by severe frosts and cold winds.*

Frost Protection

Late spring night frosts are sometimes a problem, but it is possible to protect small plants with layers of newspaper if nothing else is available, although hessian or a simple sheet of polythene will all be useful. Old curtains (even net curtains) can be draped over a vulnerable shrub or wall-trained fruit tree and although tedious to do and unsightly in appearance this may be enough to save the plant or the flowers and fruit. Whatever you use will have to be pegged or tied down, and removed in the morning. Clearly such a chore is worthwhile only to save an important crop or plant against the unexpected late frost.

garden shop or centre). It is best to measure the temperature a couple of inches below the surface for a general picture of the soil's warmth.

The following are the suggested minimum and maximum soil temperatures for sowing a range of popular vegetable seeds:

	Minimum	Maximum
Bean, broad	5°C/41°F	32°C/90°F
Bean, French	12°C/54°F	–
Bean, runner	12°C/54°F	–
Beetroot	7°C/45°F	–
Broccoli, sprouting	5°C/41°F	32°C/90°F
Brussels sprouts	5°C/41°F	32°C/90°F
Cabbage	5°C/41°F	32°C/90°F
Carrot	7°C/45°F	–
Cauliflower	10°C/50°F	32°C/90°F
Celery	10°C/50°F	19°C/66°F
Courgette	13°C/55°F	–
Cucumber, ridge	13°C/55°F	–
Kale	5°C/41°F	32°C/90°F
Kohl-rabi	5°C/41°F	32°C/90°F
Leek	5°C/41°F	22°C/72°F
Lettuce	5°C/41°F	25°C/77°F
Marrow	13°C/55°F	–
Onion	7°C/45°F	22°C/72°F
Parsnip	7°C/45°F	–
Peas	5°C/41°F	32°C/90°F
Radish	5°C/41°F	32°C/90°F
Swede	5°C/41°F	32°C/90°F
Sweet corn	10°C/50°F	–
Turnip	5°C/41°F	32°C/90°F

Most hardy annuals will germinate readily in the range 5–32°C (41–90°F) if the ground is moist. Half-hardy annuals sown outside may need higher minimum temperatures, but these are not likely to be sown outdoors until the soil has warmed up anyway.

Soil temperature is less useful as an indicator for sowing alpines and border perennials, as some of these have dormancy factors to consider (see page 81).

If you do not have a soil thermometer, it should be safe to sow most vegetables and hardy plants as soon as the buds begin to swell on the trees and shrubs.

Summer Problems

The most common summer problem is lack of rain. Natural rainfall usually provides enough water for most plants in most seasons, and watering is usually necessary only if you want to increase yield or quality of growth, or in exceptionally dry spells. Generally it is best not to water too soon during a dry spell as it may encourage surface rooting which eventually makes matters worse.

Not all crops benefit equally from irrigation. Seedlings will be among the first to suffer a severe check if the soil is too dry, but many plants will flower, and

The amount of water in the soil in summer has a marked effect on plant growth. A rain gauge is an interesting way of keeping a check on the rainfall or the amount of water delivered by a sprinkler.

possibly fruit, more prolifically in drier conditions than they will if it is wet. With some crops irrigation may simply encourage growth of the wrong parts of the plants, carrots may make more leaf but not proportionately more root for instance.

Watering – Golden Rules

● Apply adequate water to relatively few plants rather than try to do a large area skimpily. Give priority to anything newly planted.

● Once you start watering a lawn, remember that you need to continue irrigation until more rain falls. Your lawn may look unhappy in a drought, but unless it has a bowling green finish it is unlikely to suffer permanent damage by not being watered.

● Water a seedbed *before* you sow, not afterwards. Watering the drills before sowing ensures moist ground to start with and the minimum risk of washing the seeds away before they germinate.

● Be sure to keep moist any sensitive crops that will bolt (run to seed) if too dry. Chinese cabbages are a good example. Radishes will become woody if not kept constantly moist.

● In the vegetable or soft fruit garden, it will help to take out a shallow trench to one side of the row, into which you can direct water from a hosepipe or a watering can. A more elaborate variation on this is to use old lengths of plastic guttering with holes pierced along the plant side.

● For shrubs that benefit from irrigation you can form a shallow depression round the base in which water will collect (but this is not to be recommended on poorly drained soils, otherwise there will be waterlogging problems in heavy rain).

● If just a few important plants are involved, sink a plant-pot alongside the plant, and pour the water into this.

● If possible, avoid simply directing the jet of water from a hose-pipe or watering-can without a rose directly at the roots of the plants – the force of the water will often wash the soil away from the base of the plant.

● Keep weeds down – they remove more water from the ground than would be lost simply by evaporation from a bare surface.

How to water Watering with a can is tedious, but at least you can direct it to the base of the plants, where it will do most good. A hosepipe will have the same effect with less effort, but be careful to adjust the force of water so that it does not damage the soil structure or the plant. Seep hoses are also very effective. The important thing is to concentrate the water close to the plants where it will do most good.

A sprinkler is not always satisfactory because it spreads the water everywhere and not just where it will do the most good. Because it spreads it finely over both soil and foliage, more is lost through evaporation than would otherwise be the case.

It is better to water fairly intensively infrequently than to give a light sprinkling regularly (this will simply encourage surface rooting, and much of the water will be lost to evaporation before it has had a chance to penetrate). Outdoors aim to apply 2.5 cm (1 in) of water each time.

To help you estimate how much you are applying to each plant, run the water into a container of known capacity to see how long it takes to fill – then you will know how long you will need to water each plant or area. But bear in mind that mains pressure varies, and you need to have the tap turned on to the same extent each time. Aim to give crops that need it about 11 litres per sq m (2 gallons per sq yd) every week or two in hot, dry weather if the soil is sandy. Clay soils can hold more, and

Sinking a plant pot in the soil is an effective way of creating an individual reservoir.

you could double the amount and wait longer before applying more.

If you are using a sprinkler, you can easily measure how much water you are applying by inserting a rain-gauge within the area being covered.

Bear in mind that water can affect quality as well as yield. Leaf and stem vegetables such as celery will usually be more tender and succulent if kept well watered, but too much water may reduce the flavour of others – tomatoes and carrots for instance. Irrigating at the wrong time can have adverse effect: watering marrows too much too early may result in more leaves at the expense of flowers and fruit, and watering maincrop potatoes too early can encourage foliage at the expense of tubers.

Watering Equipment

Choosing the right equipment can help to make watering less of a chore. Underground pop-up sprinklers connected to a permanent pipework system is the easiest method of watering, but it is costly and is best installed during garden construction. If you water wisely, a portable sprinkler connected to a hose is perfectly adequate for most gardeners.

Sprinklers are not *necessarily* the best way to water. If you can water individual plants or rows directly with a hose fitted with a spray head, or a watering-can, the water will go where it is most needed.

Sprinklers are most useful for areas such as lawns, or perhaps a rock garden, where the whole area will benefit.

Static sprinklers are usually the cheapest – they have no moving parts and the spray is created by the pressure of water as it is forced through holes in the head. Most of them water in a circular pattern – but as few lawns or beds are circular, it is best to go for one that can be adjusted for other patterns too. This will help to avoid too many overlapping areas.

Rotating sprinklers have several arms that rotate. Covering a circular area, they suffer from the same drawbacks as most static sprinklers.

Oscillating sprinklers have the spray holes in a tube that turns or revolves. These are not usually very expensive, and they are much more versatile than the static type. It is normally possible to adjust the spray pattern or area (adjusting the tap pressure will also give some control of the area covered). This is the most useful type for most small gardens.

Pulse-jet sprinklers send out pulsating spurts over a circular area (or part of a circle). They may be more expensive than most other types, but are worth considering if you want to cover a larger area than is normally achieved with a static or rotating sprinkler. Some of them have heads on a tallish spike, which is useful if you want to place it near plants that would interfere with the jets from a sprinkler placed at ground level.

Seep hoses and spray hoses You can buy hoses with perforations that produce a fine spray along the length of the hose, which can be useful for a long, narrow lawn, but these are of limited use among growing plants because the spray is likely to be interrupted by the foliage of nearby plants.

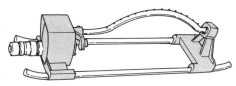

Top *Rotating sprinkler*
Above *Oscillating sprinkler*

A seep hose is useful for ensuring a constant supply of water to a relatively small number of plants, but it is not a very flexible way to water.

Seep hoses, which release the water slowly directly into the soil, are useful where they can be laid along a row of plants. As they are usually left in position, this may work out expensive (and visually unacceptable in the flower garden), but they can be very useful under cloches, or beneath a polythene mulch, where access for watering can be a problem.

Watering-can This is a basic piece of equipment. It is especially useful when planting, and is far more gentle than a hosepipe for watering containers.

For greenhouse watering choose a lighter one with a long spout and a smaller capacity. For the garden, a normal 2-gallon size can is best.

Hose with spray head A hand-held hose is ideal for watering a lot of containers, or for applying water to a lot of individual plants. But use a spray head (or even a watering-can rose pushed on the end) to break the force. The drawback of a trailing hose can be reduced by using a through-feed hose reel and hose guides at the corner of buildings or beds.

Hoses and fittings Unless you have a through-feed hose reel fitted to the outside of your house that you can just wind up after use, a hosepipe can be a problem to wind and unwind without creating kinks. The right kind of hose will make this easier, but do not assume that the fold-flat hoses that can be reeled in are necessarily the answer. You are unlikely to want to water in a straight line from the tap, and some of these kink so easily in use, blocking the flow, that they can bring their own frustrations. They are also in fixed lengths (though you can usually buy extensions), and you may find that they do not have suitable fittings

Most hoses are double-walled and some are reinforced. Reinforced hoses are the strongest and least likely to kink.

Water quality Although water butts can harbour pests and diseases, and their use for watering greenhouse plants is not without risk, there are a few plants for which rainwater may be well worth using whenever possible. If you live in a chalk or limestone area and are trying to grow acid-loving plants in containers or raised beds, the tap water may be too 'hard' (alkaline) for these plants (though by no means always so, as the water supply may come from a distant area).

For the vast majority of garden and pot plants, tap water is perfectly satisfactory.

Using Mulches

The beneficial effect of mulching on soil structure was discussed on page 32. Mulching will also reduce the need to water by reducing water loss from the soil in warm weather. A mulch will, of course, prevent light rain reaching the soil too (in the case of solid plastic no rain will get through), so it is important always to apply a mulch once the soil is thoroughly moist – preferably after a period of prolonged rain. If you mulch in late winter or in spring, it should not be difficult to find a suitable period.

Watering will still be necessary in very dry periods, but not as frequently as would otherwise be the case.

The best material for conserving moisture is black polythene or well-rotted manure or compost, but other material such as pulverized bark or peat will also help. If you use polythene wider than about 1 m (3 ft), you will probably have to use polythene layflat or seep hoses beneath the sheet. Alternatively, you may be able to water close to the stem of each individual plant, or if laid in strips either side of the crop row, water in the gap between.

Stone Mulch

Although only practical for parts of the ornamental garden, small pebbles or gravel can also be used as a moisture-conserving mulch, with the advantage of being decorative and long-lasting. Try using a black polythene mulch around shrubs and then covering this with a layer of stones or gravel – it should be trouble-free for years.

Assisting the Climate

Cloches and garden frames (often called cold frames, though you can heat them), will enable you to extend the growing season or to overwinter those plants of borderline hardiness that may otherwise be killed.

Cloches are used primarily for early protection in the vegetable garden, enabling seeds to germinate sooner in the warmer soil, and encouraging faster early growth. But they are also useful for extending the season in autumn too. Late-sown lettuces can be kept growing, for instance, and tomatoes can be kept ripening on the plant for longer. Shelter from winds can also increase yields – by as much as 25 per cent (a bigger increase than you are likely to achieve by using fertilizers for instance).

Cloches have other uses: they can provide the necessary protection for herbaceous plants and alpines that are not dependably hardy. For protection from cold each one will need an end-piece, but for plants that suffer as much from winter wetness as from the cold, the overhead protection may be enough.

Garden frames are invaluable as an adjunct to a greenhouse: they act as a half-way house for hardening off half-hardy or tender plants before planting them outside for the summer (see page 79). Without this intermediate stage the shock between the greenhouse environment and the outdoor one would probably give the plants a severe check to growth. And when the demand for space in the greenhouse is great, it is usually possible to move some plants into a frame. The garden frame is also a good home during the summer for any plants that are resting and are not decorative enough to enhance the greenhouse itself.

A garden frame is still worth considering even if you do not have a greenhouse. Many seedlings can be started a little earlier than would be possible in the open garden, and in the vegetable garden a frame can be productive the year round. For example, early varieties of lettuce, radish, and carrot can be sown in a frame and pulled early, melons and cucumbers that might not do well outdoors can be grown during the summer, and hardy lettuces can be overwintered.

Trapping Heat Radiation

Greenhouses, cloches, and frames all help plant growth simply by reducing the effect of wind (although this benefit is lost if cloches are not covered at the ends and so act as a wind tunnel), but their prime function is to trap warmth and increase soil and air temperature.

How effectively this is done depends on the glazing material (see page 53).

A garden frame can be productive the year round, but it is most valuable in spring as a half-way house between greenhouse and outdoors. Hardening off plants gradually in a frame before planting them out will ensure that they receive the minimum check to growth.

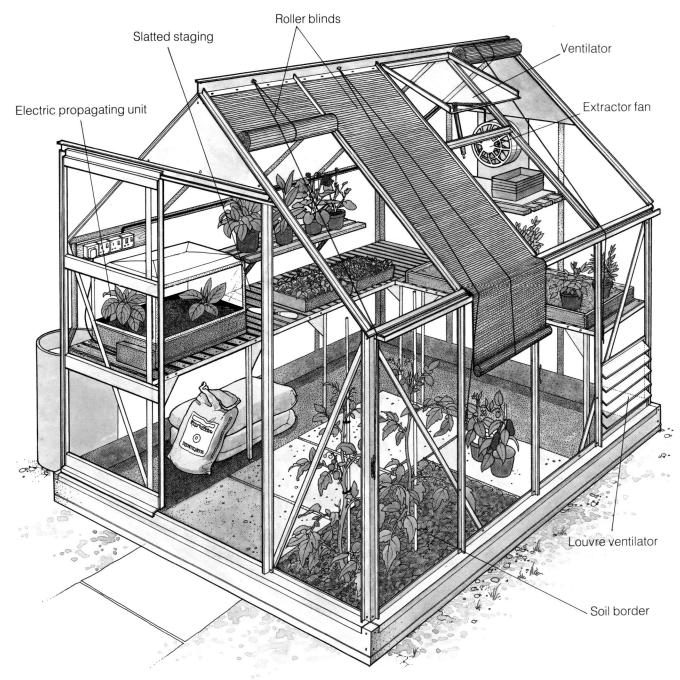

Roller blinds

Slatted staging

Ventilator

Extractor fan

Electric propagating unit

Louvre ventilator

Soil border

*A well equipped greenhouse will enable you to grow a
wide range of plants. Good ventilation is especially
important.*

The Greenhouse Microclimate

A greenhouse has its own climate, and its own problems. Although the plants are generally more protected than outdoors, heating, ventilation and lighting can all cause problems, and watering becomes an essential task not an optional one.

Temperature

The temperature in the greenhouse will be warmer than that outside, even if the structure is unheated. This is due partly to the warm air not being conducted away so quickly by wind, but primarily because of the 'greenhouse effect'. This is especially pronounced if glass is used for glazing, as it acts rather like a one-way valve. Radiant heat from the sun has a short wavelength, and passes readily through glass; but the heat that radiates back from the soil and other surfaces has a longer wavelength and does not pass so easily through glass. The result is a net increase in temperature. During the winter, in an unheated greenhouse, the difference may be small, perhaps 2–3°C (3–5°F) at night. On a sunny day the greenhouse effect will be very marked, and the problem for the plants is similar to that of an animal left in a parked and unventilated car on a hot day. The warmth that is highly beneficial when the weather is cold can be highly detrimental in excess.

Light

Although the sun warms the greenhouse air very efficiently, not all the light manages to penetrate through the glazing, and the light intensity will almost certainly be lower inside than it is outside. In summer, when shading is likely to be needed anyway, this is not especially important, but in winter when light is likely to be the limiting growth factor in a heated greenhouse, it is especially important to keep the

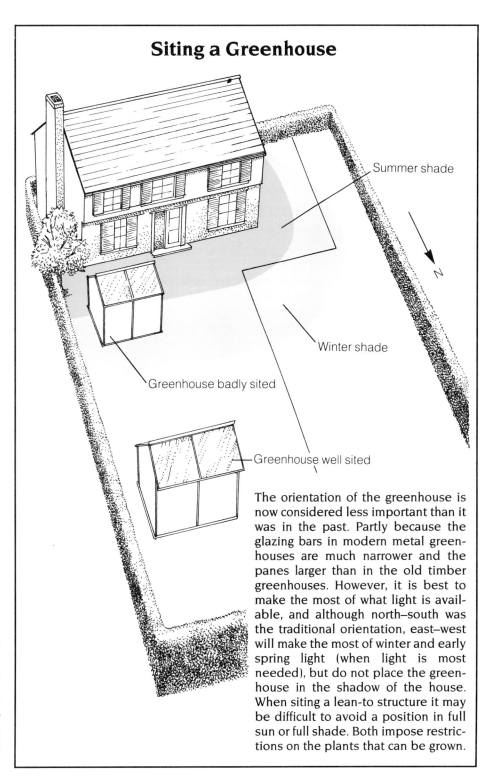

Siting a Greenhouse

Summer shade

N

Winter shade

Greenhouse badly sited

Greenhouse well sited

The orientation of the greenhouse is now considered less important than it was in the past. Partly because the glazing bars in modern metal greenhouses are much narrower and the panes larger than in the old timber greenhouses. However, it is best to make the most of what light is available, and although north–south was the traditional orientation, east–west will make the most of winter and early spring light (when light is most needed), but do not place the greenhouse in the shadow of the house. When siting a lean-to structure it may be difficult to avoid a position in full sun or full shade. Both impose restrictions on the plants that can be grown.

glazing clean, otherwise dirt and grime will cut down the already inadequate light still further.

Lack of light is unlikely to be a problem in an unheated greenhouse, or in one heated from say mid-April to mid-October, but if you are planning to heat your greenhouse during the winter it is worth checking whether it receives sufficient light to make the heating costs worthwhile. Alternatively, special lighting of a type suitable for plant growth can be installed.

Heating and Ventilation
Greenhouse heating is beyond the scope of this book, but whatever system of heating and insulation is used, you should allow for some ventilation on most days, even in winter. Otherwise the damp and stagnant atmosphere that will go with the heat will provide ideal conditions for the growth and spread of fungal diseases.

In the summer, good ventilation is crucial. It is necessary to prevent the temperature rising too high, and to prevent the relative humidity becoming too great.

Although high humidity is generally considered to be acceptable for most greenhouse plants, moderate humidity is the ideal. Plants keep themselves cool by transpiring (evaporating) water vapour from their leaves; as the relative humidity in the greenhouse rises, the rate of transpiration decreases, and the cooling effect diminishes. If the air becomes too moist, transpiration may stop, and the temperature of the plant tissue rises high enough to damage it. As botrytis and other diseases are encouraged by a relative humidity above 80 per cent, try to keep the greenhouse humidity below 75 per cent.

Because the relative humidity is affected by temperature, it is more likely to become a problem in winter if the greenhouse does not have some ventilation. The warmer the air, the more water vapour it can hold.

Providing enough ventilation to prevent overheating can be difficult. In an amateur's greenhouse there are three basic approaches to changing the air:

Extractor fans are worth considering if a power supply is available. Most are thermostatically controlled, so it is important to site the thermostat out of direct sunlight or draughts. The fan should be sited high up at one end; a louvred vent low on the opposite end will provide an inlet for fresh air (it is worth fitting an automatic louvre vent opener to this, set to open at a slightly lower temperature than the fan setting). The fan itself should have louvres that open only while the fan is running, to avoid draughts. You will need a fan able to extract at least 300 cu m an hour (10,000 cu ft an hour) for a 1.8 m × 2.4 m (6 ft × 8 ft) greenhouse if this is your only form of ventilation.

Wind-effect ventilation is achieved by at least two roof vents (on opposite sides). The external movement of air is sufficient to force fresh air in, and hot, humid air out.

Chimney-effect ventilation depends on roof vents to let the hot, humid air out, and side vents (usually louvre) low down through which the fresh air enters. This is generally a more satisfactory arrangement than wind-effect ventilation.

Few standard greenhouses have enough ventilators but you can usually buy additional ones as extras. This is almost always worthwhile. Ideally in a small greenhouse the ventilators should equal about one-sixth of the floor area for adequate ventilation, and roof ventilators should be capable of opening to an angle of 45 degrees.

No matter how many ventilators you have, the greenhouse atmosphere will still overheat if you are too slow opening them. Even if you cannot fit automatic openers to all the ventilators, fitting

them to just a few will avoid the extreme heat that can sometimes build up early on a summer's morning. If you cannot provide enough ventilation, you will have to compensate by shading.

Shading
The plants that we usually shade in a greenhouse grow perfectly happily in full sunshine outdoors. This is because outdoors the constantly changing air around them keeps the temperature lower, and the localized intense heat that results from light passing through glass, causing the leaves to scorch, does not occur.

A few plants, most cacti and succulents among them, will tolerate intense sun and heat without suffering, but most plants grown in a greenhouse need shading in summer.

Most pot plants grow best at around 15–18°C (60–65°F), although some are obviously happier with a higher temperature. If the temperature is too high, however, plants are likely to grow more slowly or the quality of growth may suffer. With crops such as tomatoes the result may be more striking: flowers may fail to set, and fruit that does set may have greenback (a form of uneven ripening).

If you do not shade, be especially careful when watering. Drops of water on the leaves can heat up rapidly in bright sunshine and cause local scorching. For that reason it is best to water in the evening, provided there is enough ventilation to prevent condensation being a problem in the morning.

It is difficult to be precise about how much shading is needed. It depends on the efficiency of the ventilation system, and of course which plants you are growing: some will naturally tolerate more intense light than others. Generally, however, shading is normally necessary from about the end of March to September in the south of Britain, and from April to August in the North, but be influenced by local conditions and the types of plant grown.

Materials vary in the amount of light that they filter. Generally something that filters about 50 per cent of the light will be the most useful. Some shading methods are used *inside* the greenhouse, but if the sun's rays have already passed through the glass much of the heat-reducing effect will have been lost, although the direct sunlight will have been filtered out for those plants that prefer shade or partial shade.

Shading applied to the *outside* helps to reduce the heat inside more effectively.

Glazing Materials

Glass is still one of the best glazing materials. It transmits about 90 per cent of the visible light, and is very efficient at trapping the long-wave radiation which helps to retain heat. Short of accidental breakage it also has a very long life. Clean the glass well in autumn as the extra light gained will be needed during the winter.

Plastics are useful but have drawbacks: the cheaper ones are not as good as glass at retaining heat, and those that are will generally be more expensive than glass.

In the protected environment of a greenhouse it is possible to grow a range of plants from many climates, as this mixed greenhouse shows. As you will usually have plants at various stages of growth, it is difficult to achieve this standard of display unless you have a second greenhouse or frames in which to keep resting or young plants.

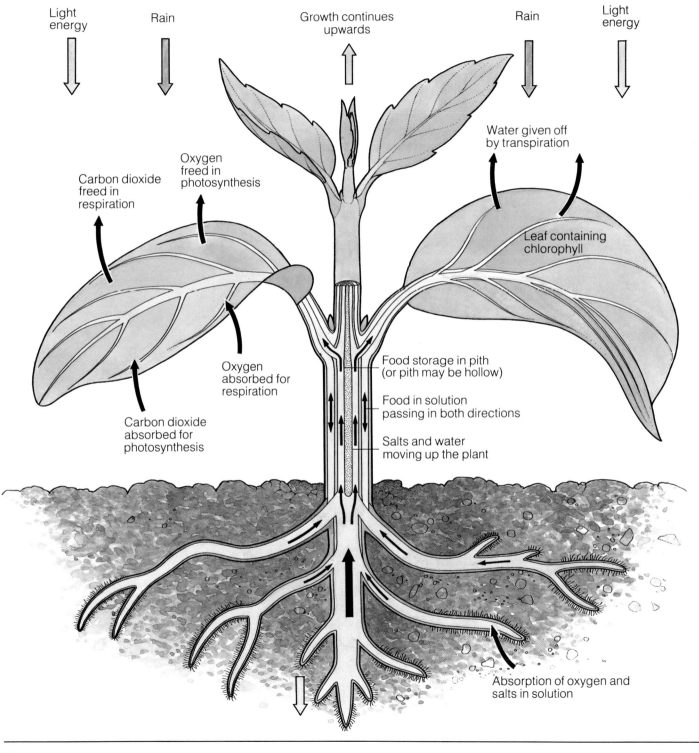

Light energy

Rain

Growth continues upwards

Rain

Light energy

Carbon dioxide freed in respiration

Oxygen freed in photosynthesis

Water given off by transpiration

Leaf containing chlorophyll

Oxygen absorbed for respiration

Food storage in pith (or pith may be hollow)

Food in solution passing in both directions

Salts and water moving up the plant

Carbon dioxide absorbed for photosynthesis

Absorption of oxygen and salts in solution

How Plants Work

You can grow good plants and have a superb garden, without the slightest knowledge of botany or the anatomy of plants. But gardening becomes even more fascinating and more successful if you understand how plants grow. Photosynthesis and respiration are complex processes, and in the explanations here they have been simplified – but it is only the principles rather than the mechanism of the processes that concern the gardener.

Photosynthesis

All green plants contain chlorophyll – a pigment which not only gives them their green colour but is responsible for extracting energy from sunlight and using it to manufacture food for the plant. It is important to realize that the nutrients supplied to the soil are only building blocks for the process of growth, and without the energy-producing products of photosynthesis the plant would die.

Even plants that look brown or red contain chlorophyll, but the greenness is masked by the presence of other pigments. The few plants that contain no chlorophyll live either as parasites or in harmony as mutually dependent plants with those containing chlorophyll (a process known as symbiosis).

During the process of photosynthesis, light energy is used to convert water taken up from the soil and carbon dioxide from the atmosphere into sugar and oxygen, the oxygen being released to the atmosphere. In the second stage of the process the sugars combine with each other and inorganic chemicals such as nitrate and phosphate to form the proteins, fats, oils and nucleic acids which are the component materials of the plant tissues.

A plant is like a self-contained chemical factory, and is capable of complex reactions.

Respiration

In this process (which continues during darkness when photosynthesis has stopped), the sugar is broken down in the presence of oxygen, energy is released and carbon dioxide and water vapour are given off through the leaves. The energy released by respiration is used by the plant for growth and other work of living.

Transpiration

This is the process by which water evaporates from the leaf, through the small pores (stomata) on the surface. As the water evaporates from the leaf cells more is drawn in from further down the plants – a knock-on effect which ultimately reaches the root.

This has several effects on plant growth; for example, in hot or windy weather the rate of transpiration increases and the plant has greater need of water. If this water is not available the plant wilts. Conditions of high humidity slow down transpiration and this means the plant has less need of water; this is the reason why cuttings are kept in a more humid atmosphere – to put less strain on a non-existent or slight root system. It is also the reason why it is necessary to slow down transpiration from newly planted subjects.

Practical Implications

The practical implications to the gardener are obvious. Most plants need plenty of light if they are to grow well; only those adapted to low light levels (these usually have large green leaves to make the best use of the available light) are likely to do well in shade or poor light. Unless the plant is naturally adapted to low light levels, no amount of feeding or watering will allow the plant to thrive: it simply will not be able to manufacture enough energy-producing food.

Light and moisture alone may not produce a thriving plant either: once the sugars have been manufactured, the other nutrients from the soil (which are usually supplied by fertilizers) must be available to be used in the later chemical reactions. And as plants depend on chemical reactions for growth, the temperature must be warm enough for these to take place. Plants sometimes grow poorly simply because it is too cold for the reactions to take place – which is obvious if seeds are sown before the soil is warm enough. In fact, seeds sown later in the spring often grow away more quickly.

Leaves

Leaves vary in size, shape, colour and texture and it is chiefly within the leaf tissues that the plant manufactures its food, the nutrients and water absorbed by the roots being passed up the stem to the leaf where chemical changes take place initiated by photosynthesis.

The leaf blade is made up of an outer skin called the epidermis which is present on both the upper and lower surfaces. In between are the leaf cells which contain small bodies called chloroplasts and these in turn contain a green pigment called chlorophyll.

In the epidermis, especially on the lower surface, are many minute holes called stomata (singular – stoma). It is through the stomata that the leaf gives off excess moisture and takes in or expels various gases.

Roots

The function of the roots is to anchor the plant in the soil and absorb nutrients and water from it. The root system comprises a main tap root which, as it grows deeper, produces lateral roots

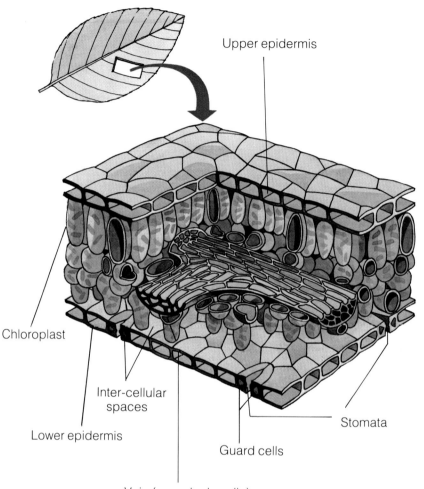

Upper epidermis

Chloroplast

Inter-cellular spaces

Lower epidermis

Guard cells

Stomata

Vein (vascular bundle)

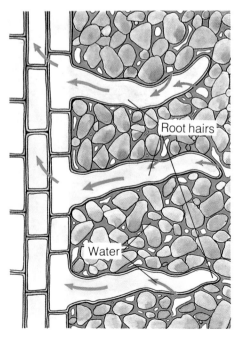

Root hairs

Water

that spread out horizontally. In this way the plant is able to exploit a large area of soil around it. But it is in the root hairs – fragile whiskers occurring just behind the root tips – that all the work is done. Here water and dissolved nutrients from the soil pass through the walls of the root hair by a process called osmosis. The amount of water in the soil will affect the ease or difficulty with which the plant can do this.

Food is stored in the roots of certain plants, such as hollyhocks and horse-radish, and it is easy to increase these by root cuttings. Root vegetables store food in their tap roots.

Osmosis This is the process by which water enters the root. The soil solution is usually much weaker in density than the solution inside the root cell and it is the movement of water from the weaker soil solution to the stronger cell solution via the membrane of the cell, that is termed osmosis. If the soil water content falls then the soil solution might become as strong as the cell solution in the root and water will no longer pass into the root's cells. If the soil loses even more water and the soil solution becomes more concentrated than that of the cell, water will actually pass out of the root into the soil. Under these conditions even with the stomata closed the plants would lose water by evaporation, and as this is not being replaced, the plant would wilt and vital processes would stop.

Stems

These form the plant skeleton as they contain thickened and strengthened cells that give the plant rigidity. Stems also provide the channels through which water and nutrients are carried from the roots to the leaves and by which the sugar produced there is carried back to where it is needed for respiration or to be stored.

Biennials are sown one year (usually in late spring or early summer) to flower the next. After flowering they usually die. Some varieties can be flowered the first year by sowing early under glass, when they behave as annuals.

Herbaceous plants have soft, rather than woody, upper growth. Most lose their top growth during the resting period (usually, but not always, winter). There are, however, evergreen non-woody plants that retain their leaves – in some cases just until new ones appear in spring (many epimediums for example), sometimes for longer.

How Long Will it Live?

Gardeners often place plants into neat, descriptive 'compartments' that are horticulturally convenient and tell us what to expect in terms of longevity, stature, and so on. But nature does not always conform to such neat labelling and a plant that might be evergreen in a favourable climate could be semi-evergreen or even deciduous in a cold area; some trees can be grown as shrubs and vice-versa; and not all herbaceous plants die down in winter. The definitions given here are the ones usually intended, but bear in mind that books and catalogues frequently give the main definition for a plant as it is grown normally in this country, even though it may not be accurate in botanical terms.

Annuals live for a single growing season then die. Usually this means they germinate in spring and die in autumn, but some can be sown to germinate in autumn and flower and die in spring or early summer (see also biennials, which are *normally* sown one year to flower the next). Removing the dead flower heads prolongs the flowering season.

Canterbury bell (Campanula medium) *is a biennial which lives for two years then dies.*

Close-up of a flower. Pollen grains (male sex cells) when deposited on the stigma produce pollen tubes which grow down through the style to fertilize the ovules (female sex cells). This fertilization results in the formation of seeds. Many flowers are specially adapted so that pollination (the movement of the pollen grains) is carried out by insects or by wind action.

Cut the top growth back in autumn. Lift, divide and replant most kinds in autumn or spring once every three years or so. Herbaceous plants can be annual, perennial, or biennial, but usually a perennial is implied.

Monocarpic plants take a variable time to reach flowering age, and die once they have fruited. Although in one sense this could apply to annuals, the term is used primarily for plants that overwinter for several seasons in a vegetative condition before flowering.

Most monocarpic plants produce offsets around the base before they die, so that the end of the parent is not necessarily the end of the plant.

Perennials live for at least three seasons (annuals live one, biennials two).

Shrubs are woody plants with many stems rather than a single main stem or trunk, although the borderline between the two is sometimes blurred. See also Trees and Sub-shrub.

Sub-shrubs are perennials with a woody framework of growth but also soft herbaceous growth that tends to die back in winter. The term is sometimes wrongly used to describe a dwarf shrub.

Trees are woody plants with a single main stem or trunk with a head of branches. Some trees may produce more than one main stem, but this is usually the result of an accident or of improper pruning or poor care.

There are, however, some plants that are commonly grown as either trees or shrubs (examples are *Amelanchier canadensis*, *A. lamarckii*, *Acer negundo*, and *Cornus mas*). In these cases it is the early training that dictates the final form, and it is important to buy a plant trained as a tree if that is what you want.

Deciduous is a term applied to a perennial plant which loses its leaves in winter and so enters a period of dormancy to enable it to survive the adverse weather conditions.

Evergreens or 'evergreys' are those plants which retain their leaves throughout the year. The leaves do, in fact, fall off and are replaced but this is a continual process and the plant is never without leaves. A plant which is evergreen in a warm climate may be semi-evergreen or deciduous in colder areas.

Bulbs, corms and tubers Some perennial plants have storage organs, usually swollen underground parts, that help them to survive their resting period (which is not always winter). These are often loosely termed 'bulbs'.

True bulbs are composed of modified leaf bases – clearly seen in a cut onion, with an embryo shoot in the centre. Most bulbs, such as tulips and narcissi, have these scales packed tightly together and encased in a tunic (a papery covering). A few bulbs lack this and the scales are more distinctly separate – lily bulbs are like this.

Corms are the thickened bases of stems, and these too are usually encased in a papery tunic. The original corm dries up during the growing period, and a new one forms above it.

Tubers are thickened sections of stem or root. Stem tubers carry several 'eyes' – clearly seen on a potato, but also present on tubers such as begonias. Root tubers, such as those of dahlias, grow only from the crown, and broken-off individual tubers will not grow.

Tubers are usually more irregular in shape than corms, but can also be distinguished by the lack of a tunic, or papery covering. Like a corm, the tissue is solid, and not made up of individual layers.

Rhizomes are perennial underground, normally horizontal, stems that produce roots and shoots at the tip as they grow away from the centre. There are several types of rhizome – the fleshy rhizomes of some irises are perhaps the best known.

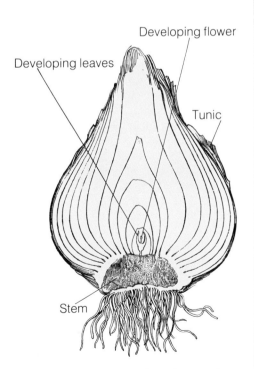

Developing flower

Developing leaves

Tunic

Stem

Above A *bulb contains an embryo plant, complete with flower if it is mature enough.*
Right Narcissus cyclamineus, *one of the easiest and most dependable of the dwarf narcissi.*

How Plants are Named

The basis of the binomial system of nomenclature used for plants was devised by an eighteenth-century Swedish botanist called Carl von Linné. It is known as the Linnaean system, after the Latin form of the botanist's name. The plant kingdom is divided into various large groupings, but to the gardener it is the specific names that matter.

Plants with enough common characteristics, even though the individual plants may look very different from each other, are put into the same family. The family name ends in -aceae, such as *Rosaceae* (rose family). Examples of plants that belong to the rose family are apricots, cherries, blackberries, raspberries, and strawberries, as well as roses. It is interesting to know to which family a plant belongs, but seldom of practical use (it can help to know whether a plant belongs to the *Ericaceae* family as these usually, but not always, require an acid soil).

The main reason for an accurate system of plant naming is so that a specific name applies to one plant only and there can be no ambiguity. In practice, however, plants are sometimes wrongly identified in commerce, and it is not unusual for plants sold by nurserymen to be wrongly identified. But this is often because they have been distributed within the trade under the wrong name rather than through any attempt to deceive.

Common names are often easy to use and can sound attractive, but of course they are usually specific to a particular country (sometimes even a region) so they cannot be international and their use can lead to confusion. *Betula pendula*, for example, is the silver birch in Britain, the European white birch in the USA, the sand or white birch in Germany. Helianthemums are rock roses to some, sun roses to others (although they do not actually belong to the rose family).

The binomial system of nomenclature is internationally recognized and overcomes this confusion.

Genus
The first part of the binomial Latin name is the generic name (singular genus, plural genera), which is equivalent to a surname. All the members of a genus (which may be as few as one or as many as hundreds) share overall characters that distinguish them from other genera. The genus is always written with a capital letter when it forms part of a full name (*Camellia japonica*). But when used collectively ('camellias and forsythias are good spring-flowering shrubs') it is usually written with a small letter.

Species
The second name is the species, abbreviated sp. (spp. for the plural). The species name is equivalent to a forename, and although the same species name may be given to plants in other genera too because they are often descriptive (*aurea* for a golden plant, *cinerea* for a grey one, *hirsuta* for a hairy one, *japonica* meaning from Japan), a particular combination of genus and species is unique and applies to no other plant.

All the species within a genus are considered to have evolved from a common ancestor, but in the course of evolution have become sufficiently distinct to breed true (although minor variations still occur).

Varieties
Many cultivated plants have an extra name after the genus and species. This is the varietal name. Sometimes variations occur that are not distinct enough to warrant the plant being considered as a separate species, even though the difference can be considerable (a pygmy form of a large conifer for instance). These may be regarded as varieties or sometimes sub-species.

This 'family tree' shows the relationship between plants in the same family, Rosaceae in this example. The top line lists a few of the many different genera which are grouped together because of botanical similarity. One of these genera, Rosa, is further broken down to show some of the main groups of roses and the position of species and varieties within the general structure.

Rosaceae FAMILY

GENERA

| Cherry (*Prunus*) | Apple (*Malus*) | Hawthorn (*Crataegus*) | Rowan (*Sorbus*) | Rose (*Rosa*) |

Wild Roses
e.g. *Rosa canina*

Old Garden Roses

Modern Garden Roses

SPECIES   *Rosa damascena* (Damask Rose)

Large-flowered (Hybrid tea)   Cluster-flowered (Floribunda)

VARIETY   *R. d.* 'Versicolor' (York and Lancaster Rose)

VARIETY   'Queen Elizabeth'

The perennial scarlet windflower, Anemone × fulgens *is a hybrid between* A. pavonina *and* A. hortensis. *Its hybrid origin is indicated by the presence of the multiplication sign in the plant name.*

Varieties can occur naturally or as a result of a breeding in cultivation. Varieties that occur in nature are given a third name (Rosa pimpinellifolia hispida), which is also written with a small initial letter. But if it occurs in cultivation, botanists call it a cultivar and write it with a capital initial letter and enclose the word or words in single quotation marks (Rosa pimpinellifolia 'William III').

The distinction between a variety that has occurred in the wild and one that has occurred in cultivation (a cultivar) is of more importance to botanists than to gardeners, most of whom use the word 'variety' to cover both kinds. This is much simpler, as the origin of a plant makes no difference to its garden value. In this book the word 'variety' has been used for both types, although typographically the correct presentation has been used.

Many of these variations occur as the result of a mutation (or change) in the genetical make up of a plant. Genes are found in all living cells and are the units of inheritance which control the appearance and growth of a plant. Occasionally during reproduction a gene is altered and this can result in a plant with slightly different characteristics. Sport is a name given by gardeners to a mutation of this kind.

Hybrids

Many garden plants are hybrids between different species. A hybrid between two species or two genera has a multiplication sign inserted when the name is printed. If the hybrid is between two species of the same genus, the × goes after the generic name: Erica × darleyensis. Sometimes the initial hybrid produces its own further variations, and these may be given varietal names: Erica × darleyensis 'Arthur Johnson'.

If the hybrid is between two genera (very much less common), the × goes before the generic name: ×Cupressocyparis leylandii.

Synonyms

Botanical synonyms result from continual botanical research. Sometimes it is decided that plants are distinct enough to be given their own genus (Cornus canadensis is now classified by some as Chamaepericlymenum canadense); sometimes plants that were once considered as distinct genera or species are later judged to be just forms of another. Names are also changed because it is discovered that the same plant was named at an earlier date by someone else (the first validly published name takes priority). For these and other reasons, plants are sometimes renamed.

It often takes many years for new names to become accepted commercially, and synonyms are usually used in gardening books and magazines only while a plant is likely to be found under either name (Viburnum farreri may also be sold as V. fragrans, for instance, and it is normal to give both names). If a plant is not yet likely to be sold under its new name (you are not likely to find the Russian vine, Polygonum baldschuanicum sold under its new name of Fallopia baldschuanica for instance), gardening books will normally use the old one to avoid confusion. The vast majority of synonyms, however, are old ones that have not been used for many years.

F_1 Hybrids

Many garden plants are already the result of hybridizing species and varieties over a long period (roses and dahlias for example), and many hybrids are propagated vegetatively. It is best to judge these plants on their merits rather than be concerned with their pedigree.

If you are sowing seeds, however, F_1 hybrids have a special significance.

F_1 stands for 'first filial' generation (the first offspring of a particular cross of two 'pure' lines). One parent might produce consistent red flowers if crossed with itself, the other white flowers if crossed with itself. Crossing the two may produce an offspring with pink flowers. The bonus to the gardener is that crossing two pure-breeding plants often results in a uniform, vigorous plant that is superior to either parent. It shows the so-called 'F$_1$ hybrid vigour'.

It is usually expensive to produce an F$_1$ hybrid because it is essential that the right pollen is transferred to the right stigmas, which may mean removing some parts of individual flowers, and perhaps pollinating each by hand. Sometimes, however, it is possible to produce parents that have only male or female flowers, in which case the job is less labour-intensive.

F$_1$ hybrids are usually superior varieties, but they are not necessarily the best to grow. F$_1$ hybrid vegetables are often bred for commercial production, where it is an advantage to have a uniform crop all available for harvesting at the same time. In your garden, it is more likely to be an advantage to have them ready for picking over a longer period.

F$_1$ hybrid seeds are generally expensive, and unfortunately you cannot save the seeds for sowing and expect the same results. Our pink-flower plant will probably produce a white-flowered plant and a red-flowered plant for every two pink-flowered offspring.

Compare the pale pink icing sugar buds of Kalmia latifolia, *the calico bush, shown above, with the deep pink blooms of the cultivar* Kalmia latifolia 'Brilliant' *on the left. These are magnificent summer-flowering shrubs for acid soils.*

Growing and Caring for Plants

The majority of plants will grow with the minimum of attention, but most will grow better if given a little extra care. Special attention when planting and while the plant is becoming established can make a significant difference to subsequent growth: and judicious pruning can make all the difference to the kind of display that some plants will produce.

Getting a Good Start

When planting annuals or seasonal bedding, it is enough to ensure that the ground is weed-free and that the position suits the plants (that sun-lovers have an open, sunny position for instance). There is no need to worry about lots of manure, and a light dressing of a general fertilizer is likely to be adequate (many annuals flower best if the ground is not too rich). When planting a tree or a shrub, however, you should take much more care – you will not get a chance to put things right the next season, and apart from lifting the plant again you have only one chance to prepare the soil well enough to see it through to maturity.

Planting a Tree or Shrub

If you are planting in a lawn, take out a circle of turf about 1 m (3 ft) across to avoid competition while the plant is becoming established, keep the area clear of growth for a season or two. If mulched with pulverized bark, for instance, the area can look quite attractive and the tree or shrub will benefit from the moisture conserved.

Plants growing in containers need constant attention to their water requirements during hot weather.

● Always dig out a hole large enough to take the roots spread out fully. Even container-grown plants should have a generous hole so that the roots are encouraged to grow outwards.

● Fork over the bottom of the hole, and if the soil is either sandy or heavy work in plenty of garden compost, well-rotted manure, or peat. Add a sprinkling of bonemeal or a general garden fertilizer. Remember to add peat and bonemeal or fertilizer to the heap of soil to be returned to the hole too.

● Try to ensure that the new soil-level matches the original depth (you can usually see the old soil-mark on the stem if the tree is bare-root). If it is difficult to determine this, plant with about 4–5 cm (1½–2 in) of soil above the highest root.

● Trees over 1.2 m (4 ft) tall when planted will need a stake – one that is one-third of the height of the tree is adequate. When a stake is used, insert it *before* returning soil to fill the hole, so that it does not damage the roots. It is a lot easier to nail a tree-tie to the stake before putting the stake into the hole.

● Spread out the roots of a bare-root plant before returning the soil, lifting the plant by the stem and moving it

When to Plant

Container-grown plants can be planted at almost any time, provided the ground is neither frozen nor waterlogged. If you plant during the summer, or during any dry spell, initially you will need to water the plant frequently.

Most bare-root and balled trees and shrubs are best planted while they are dormant, which means from late autumn to early spring. Evergreens, however, are best planted in autumn or spring.

Herbaceous plants in containers can be planted at almost any time that the soil is workable, but autumn or spring are ideal. Plants that are sometimes tricky to overwinter are best planted in spring.

Alpines are usually sold in pots and can be planted at most times, but again spring or autumn is best.

Above Position *a tree stake before you return the soil to the hole, so that you do not damage the roots.* Right A *well-planned border with plants in bold groups.*

gently up and down periodically to settle the soil between the roots. If the plant is in a container, *tease some of the roots out, and unwind any that have curled round the bottom of the pot;* if these are spread out the plant will grow out into the soil more rapidly – do not expect a pot-bound plant simply placed in a hole to do well.

● Check the planting level again before returning the last of the soil, and firm it well with your feet.

● Keep well watered until the plant is clearly becoming established, and *avoid weed competition.* Mulching (see page 32) will almost certainly pay dividends.

Planting Herbaceous Plants

Herbaceous plants bought by mail order may arrive with their roots wrapped in damp newspaper or moss and polythene (polyethylene). Always remove them from the outer wrapper as soon as possible, and cut away any diseased or damaged shoots, but do not expose the roots until you are ready to plant. Most herbaceous plants bought from shops or garden centres will be in pots.

● Prepare the ground thoroughly, being especially sure that it is free of perennial weeds that may be difficult to disentangle from the herbaceous plants later, and be generous with the manure or compost for those plants that benefit from it. All herbaceous plants are likely to respond to a dressing of a general balanced fertilizer, applied in the spring before or after planting.

● Take out holes large enough not to cramp the roots, some of which should be teased or spread out if possible.

● Refirm the soil with a fist or foot, and keep well watered until the roots have grown out into the soil. If the ground is very dry when planting, fill the hole with water first, let it drain, then plant.

● Do not plant too close together – allow space for the plants to spread.

Buying Hints

Buying by mail order can be successful, but buying from a garden centre or shop means you can select your own plants and see what you are getting. A good plant does not necessarily cost much more than a poor one, so choose carefully – a sturdy, well-grown plant will always grow away faster than one of similar size and age that has received a check to growth.

Most trees and shrubs are grown in containers, but beware of plants recently potted up (containerized plants). Lift the plant gently by the stem to make sure it does not lift out of loose compost. A *little* moss or weed growth is also a sign that the plant is established in its container, but beware: a lot of weed growth is a sign of neglect, and an absence of weeds may merely indicate that a weedkiller has been used.

Do not worry about a few roots growing through the container, but avoid any with a lot of thick roots that have grown through, or plants that have rooted into the standing ground.

Bare-root plants should have a relatively undamaged root system, which has been kept plunged in moist peat or something similar.

Balled plants (the root-ball is usually wrapped in hessian or plastic netting) should have a ball that feels firm and not crumbly, and again the plants should have the root-ball plunged in moist peat or something similar.

The problem with herbaceous plants is knowing whether they are good varieties or strains – frequently they are seed-raised which often means variable results, and labelling is sometimes imprecise.

Try to buy only well-labelled plants that look established in their containers (plants with peat-protected or moss-wrapped roots can be satisfactory provided the growth is not too advanced).

Rock plants should look well established, but check that they are not pot-

The caraway plant on the left, bought by mail order, is already showing signs of starvation; the one on the right, bought from a garden centre for about the same price, is a much stronger plant that has been kept growing vigorously. Purchasing from a garden centre gives you the chance to see if you are buying a healthy plant.

bound. Poor labelling, or weathered labels, are often an indication of neglect. Always check the compost – don't buy if it has been allowed to dry out.

Keeping Plants Happy

Although they will grow without, most plants will benefit from feeding occasionally. This will help them to grow more lushly or flower more prolifically, and bulbous plants, for example, will probably do better in future years. It is possible to buy fertilizers specially formulated for particular plants, such as roses or chrysanthemums, but if you want to keep things simple just use a general fertilizer containing N, P, K (see page 28) once a year, twice for vigorous or fast-growing plants. Follow the application rates suggested on the packet.

Concentrate feeding and mulching (see page 32) on newly planted or young plants; an established shrub

Rules for Applying Fertilizers

- Never guess at amounts to use, overdoses can be harmful, too little may be ineffective.
- Always follow manufacturer's instructions
- Always apply evenly
- Never mix fertilizers together unless you are sure it is safe to do so
- Never apply liquid fertilizer to dry soil or composts. Always water first
- Do not allow fertilizer to touch leaves or flowers, unless, of course, it is a foliar feed
- For a base dressing apply before sowing or planting and rake or hoe into the top few inches of soil
- For a topdressing sprinkle the fertilizer on the soil around plants during the growing season

border and established trees should not require routine feeding, although they will still benefit from an annual mulch of compost if you have any available.

A general balanced fertilizer is adequate for most garden plants, including the lawn, the vegetable plot, and fruit, and buying a larger quantity of one fertilizer should reduce the cost.

Special Fertilizers

Although general fertilizers are adequate for the vast majority of plants, there are circumstances in which it is worth using a special fertilizer. A foliar feed is especially useful to help get a plant off to a good start if it has received a check to growth. It is even worth foliar feeding a newly-planted hedge if it seems to need an extra initial boost.

It is also worth foliar feeding plants that are recovering from a serious setback caused by a pest or disease. One containing growth stimulants can be especially useful.

If the plants are suffering from a mineral deficiency, it may be necessary to use an appropriate fertilizer or trace element (see page 28). If the deficiency is induced by an alkaline soil causing iron or other elements to become unavailable to the plant, the plants will need to be treated with a special chelated product (it may be described as Sequestrene), see page 19.

Nutrient Deficiency Symptoms

Plants need a number of chemical substances with which to build up their stems, leaves, flowers and fruit, but from a practical viewpoint the first three mentioned here are the most important.

Nitrogen N Encourages good and rapid growth. Without it growth will be poor, foliage may be yellowish and leaves reduced in size. Too much delays plants reaching their flowering and fruiting stages.

Potassium (Potash) K A growth stimulant, giving general hardiness, disease resistance and vigour. Lack shows up as browning and scorching of leaf tips and edges, starting first on the oldest leaves. Fruit ripens unevenly.

Phosphorus P Encourages good root formation, stimulates flowering and encourages fruit setting. A need for phosphorus shows as dull poor growth with blue-green or purple leaves. Older leaves are affected first.

Calcium (Lime) Ca This improves the structure of heavy soils and helps the biological processes. It is a constituent of cell walls. Lack of calcium is indicated by tips of young leaves curling inwards and scorching. Dark spots in flesh and on skin of fruits. Central leaves of celery blacken.

Iron Fe At its most deficient on chalky soils. Leaves become yellow with veins remaining dark green. Youngest leaves affected first.

Manganese Mn Lack of this element is likely to be a problem on badly drained soils and shows as a yellowing of the leaves between the veins. Similar to iron deficiency but starting first on older leaves.

Magnesium Mg Deficiency common on light, sandy, acid soils. Lack shows as a yellowish marbling between the veins, starting on older leaves first.

Boron Bo Deficiency symptoms similar to those of calcium on young leaves. Rough patches on apples and root vegetables. Deficiency most likely on sandy or chalky soils.

Molybdenum Mo Mostly a problem on acid soils and with brassica plants. Leaves imperfectly developed, younger leaves strap shaped. Deficiencies are often cured by liming.

Pruning

Pruning techniques can baffle even experienced gardeners, and it is easy to do more harm than good if you wield the secateurs too enthusiastically.

Rather than try to learn specific techniques for particular plants, it is best to start by understanding the principles of pruning and the ways in which pruning can modify growth. Guided by these principles you should be able to tackle most pruning jobs even if you have not dealt with that particular plant before.

Growth and Its Control

The illustration shows that leaves and buds arise at points on the stem known as nodes, and the sections of stem between them are called internodes.

The apical buds are the ones at the end of each shoot, while those that arise from the leaf axils (the angle between a leaf and the stem) are known as axillary buds. The apical buds are best thought of as undeveloped branches waiting to grow in response to the correct stimulus. Some buds will produce flowers instead of shoots.

If you are pruning a dormant plant, start by observing the arrangement of buds on the stems. Some buds are arranged in opposite pairs, while on other plants they are arranged alternately. If you prune back to a bud where they are arranged in opposite pairs, the plant will produce a pair of branches at that point; if the buds are alternate a new branch will form on the side and in the direction of the bud. If there is a markedly dominant apical bud with a large number of dormant (very small and undeveloped) axillary buds, you can expect the branches to be elongated with few side-shoots; if there are plenty of active axillary buds, you can expect the shoots to elongate relatively slowly but to have plenty of quite fast-growing side branches. This will help you to anticipate the resulting shape of the plant after pruning.

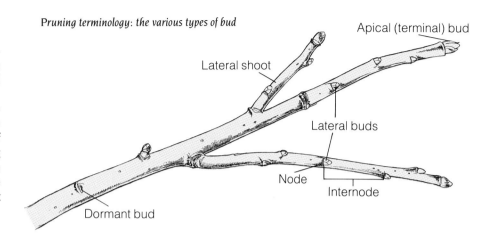

Pruning terminology: the various types of bud

Apical (terminal) bud
Lateral shoot
Lateral buds
Node
Internode
Dormant bud

Right and wrong ways to prune

Correct
Make a clean cut just above a bud and sloping away from it.

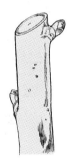

Wrong
Do not make the cut too far above a bud. The snag left will be starved of sap and will die. Infection may then spread down the branch.

Wrong
Do not make the cut so that it slopes towards the bud. This will allow rainwater to collect around the bud and rot it.

Wrong
Do not cut too close to the bud as there is a risk of damaging it.

Wrong
A ragged cut is the result of using blunt secateurs. Damaging the branch in this way provides a large area over which infection can enter the tissues.

Secateurs

If you have a lot of shrubs or fruit trees to prune regularly, it is worth investing in a good pair of heavy-duty secateurs. If you have only light pruning to do occasionally, general-purpose or light duty secateurs should be adequate.

There are three main types, described here, but more important than the cutting action is how comfortable they are to use. Try them in the hand *in an open position* to make sure you can hold them comfortably. The shape of the handle as well as the extent to which the handles open, and the strength of the spring, can all affect ease and comfort of use. Make sure they are not top-heavy, and if they feel heavy in the shop, you will probably find them tiring to use.

If you are left handed, you can use them simply by turning them round, but then the catch may be difficult to manage – so make sure you can operate the catch easily.

A good pair of secateurs should be capable of making a clean cut without bruising or tearing the stem.

By-pass (scissor-action) secateurs have a sharpened blade that cuts against a squared blade. One blade has a convex shape the other concave. This type is shown in the illustration on the near left.

Anvil secateurs have a blade that cuts against a flat anvil (sometimes with a slight groove in it). There are several variations in cutting action (some blades slice through rather than press through the stem). This type is shown on the far left.

Parrot-beak secateurs have a scissor-like action but both blades are convex and usually sharpened.

Apical dominance This expression means that the apical bud is physiologically more active than the lateral buds, which either grow more slowly or remain dormant. The apical bud produces an auxin (hormone) which subdues the axillary buds, but once the apical bud with its supply of auxin is removed the buds below can grow more freely and in turn they establish apical dominance. Even if the dominant bud can be induced to grow more slowly it may reduce the production of the auxin enough to allow lateral buds to break dormancy. This is what happens when the main branch of a young tree is forced to grow in a horizontal position, a phenomenon exploited in the training of some fruit trees.

If you bear in mind the effect of apical dominance you will appreciate that cutting the top of the branches of an over-vigorous or large tree will not solve the problem – more shoots will take over and the problem may eventually become worse. It is far better to remove a whole branch rather than simply remove the upper portion of it if you want to control the overall size.

Pruning Ornamentals
Trees should need very little routine pruning once they are established. During the formative years you can remove some young lateral branches if you want a clear stem to a certain height, otherwise confine surgery to cutting out any dead, dying, or diseased

wood. Pruning a large established tree is beyond the scope of this book, and this potentially hazardous job is best left to a professional tree surgeon.

Conifers, especially, should be pruned with restraint (unless you are growing a suitable hedging species). Few of them carry dormant buds on the woody parts of the stems and branches, which means that if you cut into mature wood no regeneration takes place (yew is an exception and this will usually shoot again even if cut back hard). A conifer can easily look mutilated.

Most shrubs will also grow well with the minimum of routine pruning, but always cut out any dead or diseased shoots when you notice them, and it may be necessary to remove any branches that are encroaching on other plants or over a path (though you should have regard to the symmetry of the bush when doing this). If you have to keep hacking back a shrub because it is too large, it was the wrong choice in the first place and may be it would be better to remove it.

There are, however, shrubs that will look better, and flower better, if pruned routinely. Examples of pruning methods for some popular shrubs are given below; the lists cannot be comprehensive, but if you follow the principles outlined you should be able to decide how to prune any other shrubs in your garden.

The vast majority of shrubs that need pruning fall into one of the following groups:

Deciduous, early-flowering Shrubs that flower in spring and early summer usually flower on shoots produced during the previous season, so careful timing is essential with this group. If you prune in winter or very early spring, you will be cutting out this year's flowers. Prune these shrubs soon after flowering, but do not wait too long as you should allow plenty of time for shoots to grow to carry next year's flowers.

PLANTS TO PRUNE	
Ceanothus*	Philadelphus
Corylopsis	Ribes
Cytisus*	Spiraea arguta
Deutzia	S. thunbergii
Forsythia	S. × vanhouttei
Jasminum nudiflorum	Weigela
Lilac	
*Spring flowering spp.	

WHAT TO DO

● Cut out dead, diseased, or crossing branches.

● Remove any branches that are spoiling the shape or symmetry.

● Thin out the oldest and very weak branches, to leave space for young, vigorous shoots to develop properly. Do not remove all the old wood.

● Cut back flowered wood by between a third and two-thirds.

Pruning may not be necessary every year, so do not worry if you miss for a year if the plant is healthy and has a good shape.

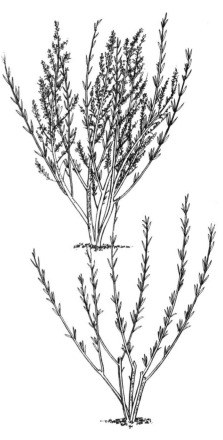

Above Most *deciduous early-flowering shrubs can be pruned by cutting back the shoots by between a third and two-thirds, soon after flowering has finished.*
Left The *graceful arching flowering sprays of* Spiraea thunbergii. *This early-flowering shrub should be pruned immediately after flowering.*

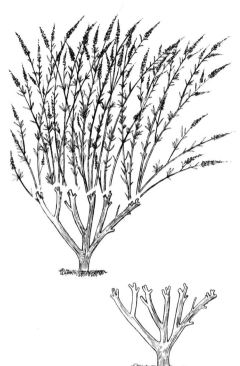

Deciduous shrubs that flower from mid-summer onwards on shoots produced during the current season are generally pruned just before they come into growth in spring. Most of them can have the shoots cut back to a woody framework 60–90 cm (2–3 ft) high (but see text). The Buddleia davidii illustrated is pruned harder than most of the others.

Deciduous, late-flowering Deciduous shrubs that flower from July onwards usually flower on shoots produced during the current season. Pruning should therefore be timed to give the shrub as long as possible to produce plenty of new shoots. Prune them in March, just before they start into growth.

PLANTS TO PRUNE	
Buddleia davidii	*Hydrangea paniculata*
Caryopteris	Roses (shrub)
Ceanothus azureus	*Spiraea × bumalda*
Fuchsia (hardy)	Tamarix

WHAT TO DO

● If the plant produces a lot of herbaceous-type growth and tends to die back (such as fuchsias and *Spiraea × bumalda*), cut the growth back to ground level.

● If there is normally a woody framework of old branches, cut the shoots back to this framework – most can be cut back to a framework about 60–90 cm (2–3 ft) high.

The plants listed above benefit from annual pruning, but some late-flowering deciduous shrubs (the Lacecap and Hortensia hydrangeas for instance) need little pruning, and others (such as Buddleia alternifolia) need no more than dead wood removed and a little thinning.

Evergreens No evergreen requires hard pruning, and small shrubs such as hebes and rosemary are unlikely to need any routine pruning. If they look dead after a hard winter, wait until May before cutting them back, then you can see which parts are going to shoot.

WHAT TO DO

● If the plant has large or conspicuous flowers, such as rhododendrons, it is worth removing the dead flower heads to improve the appearance, but avoid damaging the new shoots that grow from behind the flower heads of plants such as rhododendrons.

● Heaths and heathers are best clipped over with shears after flowering to improve the appearance and to keep the plants compact and bushy. Avoid cutting back into old wood. October is a good time to clip over summer-flowering varieties. April or May is best for winter-flowering kinds.

● Grey-leaved evergreens are usually cut back to within a couple of nodes of the previous year's growth in spring, to maintain an abundance of foliage.

● Some variegated evergreens may gradually revert to green unless shoots with all-green leaves are cut out. Do this as soon as any are noticed.

Wall shrubs These require training as well as pruning. One of the most effective methods of training is to fix horizontal wires about 45 cm (1½ ft) apart and tie the branches to these. It will take several years to form a good framework, but pruning is simple – just tie in sideshoots that arise in the correct place and cut out the others in between, and any outward-pointing shoots. Once a good framework has been formed, allow shoots to fill in the gaps but cut out shoots that are growing outwards away from the framework or inwards towards the wall.

Some shrubs, such as chaenomeles are not easily trained to horizontal wires, and these are best treated as fans. With chaenomeles, cut back all new growth to three or four leaves after flowering. Further pruning will be required in autumn, when subsequent growth should be trimmed back to two buds. Pyracanthas should have wood that has fruited thinned to well-placed shoots; to control growth further, pinch out shoots just outside the outermost flower clusters in summer.

The best time to prune wall-trained shrubs is whenever you would prune them as free-standing plants. Evergreens, such as evergreen ceanothus are best pruned after flowering.

Climbers Self-clinging climbers, such as the Virginia creeper and ivies, need no special training – simply cut back areas that are becoming overgrown.

Honeysuckles and similar vigorous twining climbers are best contained by cutting out a portion of old wood after flowering (see under clematis), and thinning if required.

Wisteria can present problems, and there are several methods. To keep the plant reasonably compact, and to promote good flowering, prune in August by cutting back the current season's branches to within 15 cm (6 in) of their point of origin. Then in winter, cut the spurs back further to a dormant flower bud (these are fatter than leaf buds).

Coping with Clematis

Clematis are among the most confusing climbers to prune, because the method of pruning depends on the type.

Flowering in mid and late spring (such as C. *montana* and C. *macropetala*) should be pruned after flowering (if pruned in winter, you will be cutting off the flower buds). Simply remove any overgrown sections.

Producing large flowers in early summer (such as 'Nelly Moser' and 'Lasurstern') also produce flowers on the previous year's growth. They need little pruning other than trimming back shoots that have flowered, if necessary, immediately after flowering. A neglected plant can be pruned hard in late winter but you will sacrifice the next flush of flowers.

Flowering in mid and late summer (such as 'Jackmanii' and the Viticella clematis) respond to hard pruning in late winter or early spring. Cut them back to within about 1 m (3 ft) of the ground.

If you are in doubt about which group a variety belongs to, check the label when you buy it, or look in clematis catalogues – these will usually tell you when to prune.

'Nelly Moser' blooms in early summer.

Cornus alba '*Sibirica*', *one of the dogwoods coppiced for its attractive winter stems.*

Coppiced shrubs Some shrubs are grown for their colourful winter stems, some coppiced shrubs for their large or attractive summer foliage. They will all grow satisfactorily without annual pruning, but the effect may be less attractive. If you do not want to cut the shrub back every year, try doing it every second or third year.

PLANTS TO PRUNE FOR STEM EFFECT
Cornus alba
C. stolonifera 'Flaviramea'
Salix alba 'Chermesina' and 'Vitellina'
Rubus cockburnianus

PLANTS TO PRUNE FOR FOLIAGE EFFECT
Cotinus coggygria
Paulownia tomentosa
Eucalyptus (will produce juvenile foliage if treated this way)

WHAT TO DO
The plants grown primarily for their decorative winter stems should have old stems cut back close to ground level in early spring as it is the newest shoots that usually have the best colouring, and it keeps the plants compact.

Eucalyptus (they become shrub-like treated this way) can be cut back to a framework of the required height in spring. Doing this regularly not only keeps the plant compact but ensures that juvenile foliage is produced (this is more attractive than mature foliage for cutting). Juvenile leaves are rounded, adult leaves are elongated.

Paulownias have especially large leaves if the previous year's stems are cut almost to ground level in early spring.

Pruning roses It does not really matter whether roses are pruned in autumn or spring, though in cold areas spring is probably better; in any case be prepared to remove any sections killed or damaged during the winter.

There are various pruning techniques for roses – the one described here is moderate pruning, which is suitable for most established large-flowered (hybrid tea) and cluster-flowered (floribunda) roses. Newly-planted roses are usually pruned harder to establish a good framework.

WHAT TO DO
● Start by cutting out completely any diseased or damaged shoots, and remove any crossing or overcrowded stems in the centre. Also remove any stems that have been flowering poorly.

● Shorten the remaining stems by about half their length. Some people prefer to leave some stems unpruned on cluster-flowered roses to spread the flowering season; make sure these stems are pruned back the following year. If there are any very weak shoots, cut these back harder – to about a quarter of their original length.

Pruning fruit Fruit trees and soft fruits such as raspberries need thoughtful pruning if you are to get the best crop, and the initial formative pruning is often different to the routine pruning for established plants. As the method of pruning can vary not only with the type of fruit but also with the method of training, it is worth consulting a specialist fruit book, where there is space to illustrate the techniques in detail.

Propagation

Raising your own plants is a very satisfying aspect of gardening.

Plants can be increased in two main ways, either sexually by seed or asexually by any of the vegetative methods – cuttings, layers, budding or grafting, and so on. In the case of plants produced from seed, the progeny may or may not resemble the parent plant closely, see F_1 hybrid (page 62). But vegetatively produced plants are always identical to the parent from which they are taken. All the plants produced by vegetative propagation from one plant make up a *clone*.

Useful Equipment

A propagator, either heated or unheated, will speed up the process of rooting or seed germination. It does this by providing a microclimate which will be warmer and more humid than the outside air. High humidity is important as it slows down transpiration until the new plant forms a big enough root system to cope with water uptake. If you are germinating only a few seeds or rooting a few cuttings, substitute a pot and a large polythene bag.

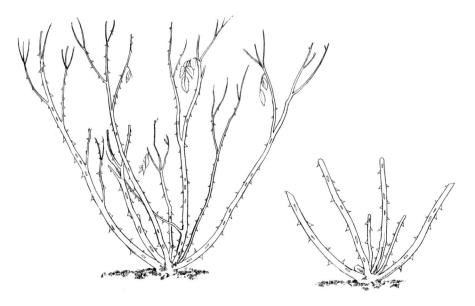

Established roses are easy to prune – if you're unsure, just cut out any damaged or diseased stems, then cut the remaining shoots back by half their length. Weak shoots should be cut back further, and on cluster-flowered (floribunda) roses you can leave some stems unpruned to spread the period of flower.

Seeds Each seed is produced by the fertilization of an ovule by a pollen cell and it contains within it a complete embryonic plant together with a supply of reserve food materials. The food stored is sufficient to last the embryonic plant through germination and until the leaves start to manufacture food for themselves. In some seeds, e.g. the cereal crops, the stored food provides a staple diet for animals too.

The length of time that seeds remain viable varies with the type of seed and the way it is stored. Try to keep them cool and protected from mice.

Vegetative methods These depend for their success on the fact that a part of a plant can often reproduce the whole by growing the missing pieces. A stem cutting consisting of stem, buds and leaves will produce a root system, for example. Similarly, a root cutting consisting of a piece of root only will develop growth buds.

Methods It is not possible to cover all aspects of propagation in one chapter of a general book, but the principles described here should enable you to propagate the majority of plants easily. Grafting and budding are techniques not described as they are much more useful commercially than they are to an amateur, who may well have the problem of obtaining suitable rootstocks and grafting or budding material.

Bear in mind that many plants can be propagated by more than one method; your choice may be different to that of a commercial grower because he needs the maximum number of plants, you may need relatively few.

Taking Softwood Stem Cuttings
Softwood cuttings are not necessarily 'woody' at all. The term is used to describe young shoots that have not yet hardened and become woody; it covers the young shoots of shrubby plants, but also herbaceous plant cuttings too.

WHAT TO DO
● Take the cuttings when the plant is growing vigorously (usually spring). Make the cuttings a few inches long (they can be smaller or larger, it depends on the plant), cutting them just below a leaf joint with a *sharp* knife.

● Remove the lower leaves as these are likely to rot if buried, and may affect the stem. And if necessary dip the base into a rooting hormone.

● If you have a propagator, insert the cuttings around the edge of a pot; if you have to use a polythene bag instead of a propagator, place several cuttings towards the centre of the pot, so that they are not in contact with the polythene. If you are not using a rooting preparation containing a fungicide, dip the cutting into a fungicidal solution anyway. It is especially important to maintain a humid atmosphere while softwood cuttings root, and this encourages fungal diseases.

● Either place the cuttings in a propagator or enclose the pot of cuttings in a polythene bag, supported on canes or wires to keep it off the cuttings. Keep in a lightly shaded position until rooted (which is usually within weeks). Mist once a week with a fungicide.

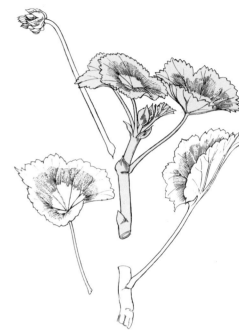

Softwood cuttings are always taken from young growth. Trim the stem and remove lower leaves and flower buds.

Rooting Hormones

Hormone rooting preparations contain chemicals that are copies of natural growth regulators. The two most commonly used are indole butyric acid (IBA) and naphthylacetic acid (NAA). They are most often sold as powders in which the chemical is mixed with a carrier such as talcum powder, French chalk, or China clay. IBA is likely to be the best choice for a wide range of plants, though some respond to NAA. Neither should be used on leaf or root cuttings.

Do not over-apply a rooting hormone – it may stimulate roots, but when they emerge and come into contact with the chemical their development can be arrested. Apply it to the very tip only (most is absorbed through the cut surface anyway). Dipping the end in water first will help more powder to adhere to the cut end. Use a dibber to insert the cuttings, otherwise the powder may be rubbed off when you push the cutting into the compost.

Semi-hardwood and Hardwood Cuttings

These cuttings are also known as semi-ripe and ripe cuttings. Semi-hardwood cuttings are commonly used for propagating evergreen trees and shrubs, and should be taken when the young shoots begin to harden at the base. Hardwood cuttings are usually taken between mid-autumn and late winter (just at or after leaf-fall is a good time) and are commonly used for deciduous trees and shrubs.

WHAT TO DO

● Try to choose vigorous shoots that are neither too old nor too young. Use a sharp knife, or secateurs, making most semi-hardwood cuttings about 5–15 cm (2–6 in) long, and most hardwood cuttings about 15–23 cm (6–9 in) long. The length will vary with the plant.

● Trim off the lower leaves, and if you have had difficulty with rooting a particular plant before, try removing a slice of bark, an inch or so long, on one side of the base. This injury helps some cuttings to root, though the exact reason is not fully understood.

● Dip the whole cutting in a fungicidal solution – using waterproof gloves – then the base into a rooting hormone. Some may root just as well without the hormone, but most hardwood cuttings will benefit.

● Semi-hardwood and hardwood cuttings can be rooted in a propagator, a garden frame, or in a pot indoors (see softwood cuttings), and this is probably the best method for most evergreens. Hardwood cuttings of deciduous plants are usually rooted outdoors (in a garden frame or the open ground). Using a spade, make a slit with a vertical face and a sloping side, and sprinkle some sharp sand along the bottom. Insert the cuttings, resting them against the vertical face, about 8–15 cm (3–6 in) apart, and return the soil, firming lightly. If the cuttings are dormant, make a sloping cut at the top so that you know which way to insert them.

Above Hardwood cuttings can be rooted outdoors. Left All kinds of cuttings are best dipped into a normal strength fungicidal solution, but use gloves.

Root Cuttings

A few plants can be raised very successfully from root cuttings, but they must be taken when the plant is dormant (mid or late winter is usually the best time). Plants to try this way include *Primula denticulata*, *Pulsatilla vulgaris*, border poppies, border phlox, and verbascum.

WHAT TO DO

● Lift the dormant plant and wash the roots, then cut off suitable young roots close to the crown. Return the parent plant to the ground.

● Use only undamaged roots and remove any fibrous lateral roots. You may be able to make several cuttings from one root. If the cuttings are being planted outdoors, they need to be about 10 cm (4 in) long, but if they are to be rooted in a propagator or indoors, they need only be about 5 cm (2 in) long.

● It is usual to make a horizontal cut at the top of each cutting, and a sloping cut at the bottom – so that you do not make the mistake of planting them wrong way up.

Simple Layering

There are several forms of layering, but simple layering is the best to choose if you just want to increase a suitable garden shrub by one or two plants.

WHAT TO DO

● Choose a vigorous sideshoot that you can bend down easily to bring it into contact with the soil. Wounding the stem at the point of contact often helps rooting. There are various ways of doing this: two of the easiest are to twist the stem or to make an angled cut half way through the stem, and wedge it open with a piece of matchstick.

● Make a shallow trench with a straight back and a slope towards the parent plant. Bend the stem at right angles about 23 cm (9 in) behind the tip, and peg it down so that the wounded portion is in the trench.

● Return the good soil to the trench (use a potting compost if the soil is poor), and keep well watered. When the plant has rooted – probably in the autumn if layered in spring – sever it from the parent plant and lift about a month later.

Below left *Root cuttings are easy if you take them at the right time (mid or late winter); at other times of year good results are unlikely.*
Below *Layering is an excellent way to propagate one or two more shrubs. It's worth trying it with most shrubs if there is a low-growing branch that you can peg to the ground.*

● Thick roots are best inserted vertically, with the top of the root just beneath the surface. Plants such as phlox produce thinner roots and these are best placed horizontally on the compost and covered with a thin layer of compost.

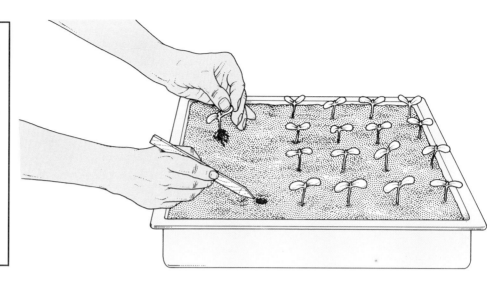

Composts for Cuttings

Compost structure is more important than the nutrients it contains. Cuttings do not need nutrients until they have rooted and are ready for potting up. What they need to root effectively is a moist yet open compost with plenty of air. You can buy suitable composts or you can make your own from equal parts of sieved peat and sand (⅛–¹⁄₁₆ grade). Vermiculite and perlite (on their own or mixed) are clean and extremely efficient for rooting cuttings.

Sowing Indoors

Most pot plants and half-hardy bedding plants and tender vegetables have to be raised under glass or in the home. Unless you have a warm greenhouse you will have to use a propagator or wait until you can maintain 13°C (55°F) or more before it is worth sowing most seeds; ideally it should be much warmer. Indoors it is likely to be warm enough, but do not sow too early in the year unless you can provide a light windowsill and additional lighting.

WHAT TO DO
● Use clean containers (pots for a few seeds, trays for a lot), and fill them with moist seed compost. Use a piece of wood, or the base of a jam jar, and firm the compost gently (do not over-firm a peat-based compost).

● Sow *evenly*. Time spent sowing thinly will save more time when pricking out. Most seeds are best covered with their own depth of compost, but a few seeds need light to germinate and should not be covered.

● If the seeds are large, water with a fine-rosed watering-can, otherwise stand the container in a bowl of shallow water until the moisture seeps through to the surface, then allow to drain.

● If you are not using a propagator, cover the pot or tray with a piece of glass or polythene to conserve moisture, and cover this with sheets of brown paper or newspaper unless you know that the seeds require light. Turn the glass daily to avoid condensation drips, and remove both paper and glass as soon as the seeds start to germinate, but protect from hot sun. Turn the pots daily if they are on a windowledge.

● Prick off the seedlings before they become overcrowded. Always handle them by the seed leaves. Use a potting compost and space the seedlings about 5 cm (2 in) apart, or put them into small individual pots.

Hardening Off

When raising half-hardy plants indoors *always* harden them off carefully before planting outdoors. If you have a garden frame, use this, gradually leaving the lights (tops) off for longer and longer periods, at first during the daytime only. Otherwise stand the plants outside on warm days and bring them in at night, then leave them out on warm nights. Do not plant out frost-tender plants (or leave them outside without protection overnight) until danger of frost is past.

Always prick out seedlings to give them more space to grow, before they become too crowded. Be guided by the plant – the smaller the seedling the longer you may have to wait to handle it easily – but as a guide aim to prick them out as soon as the first true leaf has formed (with most plants this will have a different appearance from the first leaves to open).

Sowing Outdoors

Most vegetable and hardy annuals are sown outdoors. But do not be in too much of a hurry to get them sown in spring – later sowings often catch up earlier ones that have received a check to growth from the cold. If you are sowing hardy annuals, it is best to do so in drills rather than broadcast, as it will be easier to weed between the rows, and you can distinguish between weeds and the sown plants more readily at an early stage. If the rows are close together the plants will merge into each other anyway.

Although most vegetables and hardy annuals are sown where they are to grow, some are sown in a seedbed, possibly transplanted into a nursery bed, and moved to their final positions later. This generally saves space as they occupy less ground during the early stages of growth.

Biennials, such as wallflowers and forget-me-nots, are usually sown in a seedbed in late spring or early summer, moved to a nursery bed (a summer area where they can be grown fairly close together), and planted out in autumn.

WHAT TO DO
● Always sow on well-prepared ground that has been cleared of perennial weeds and left long enough for annual weeds to have germinated and been killed. Take out drills deep enough to cover the seed with once or twice their own depth of soil, unless otherwise recommended on the packet.

● Unless the ground is already moist, water the drill thoroughly *before* sowing (heavy watering afterwards may wash the seeds about).

● Sow *thinly* unless you know that the germination is likely to be poor. Time spent sowing carefully will save much more time thinning later. If you find sowing evenly difficult, try using a seed sower or use pelleted seed.

● Rake the soil level without disturbing the rows, and keep watered during dry spells until the seedlings have emerged and are growing well.

● Thin early. Go by the recommendation on the packet for final spacing. Never thin to the final spacing in one go, just in case natural losses occur; thin to half the final spacing first.

Fluid Sowing

This is a technique used to get early vegetables off to a good start (you could use the method for difficult flowers too).

The advantages of fluid sowing are that you can germinate the seeds quickly under more controlled conditions and when you then 'sow' them outdoors you *know* that they have germinated. The seedlings should also get off to a quick, even start.

There should also be less thinning to do, *provided you can judge the delivery rate adequately.*

Do not expect fluid sowing to make much difference when you can sow outdoors in moist soil when the weather is warm – the main advantage is for early or difficult-to-germinate crops.

Vegetable seeds are sown in drills which are drawn out with the edge of a hoe or a piece of stick. Large seeds, such as the beans illustrated here, are individually positioned.

WHAT TO DO

Kits are available containing all the equipment and materials (except seed) needed, but it is easy to improvise.

● Sow the seeds evenly on several layers of damp kitchen roll in a container such as a plastic sandwich box. Let excess water drain before sowing.

● Put the lid on the box and keep it in a warm place, such as an airing cupboard (only a few kinds, such as celery are best in light), but check them twice a day.

● When the seeds have germinated, but before the roots grow more than about 2 mm (1/10 in) long, prepare the sowing gel.

● Mix about 10–20 ml (2–4 teaspoons) of cellulose wallpaper paste (no fungicide) for every metre (yard) to be sown. As a guide, use a heaped teaspoonful of the powder to 250 ml/½ pt of water, although you may have to adjust this if it is too stiff or too runny.

● Once the paste has stood long enough to thicken, gently wash the seeds off the paper into a fine-mesh sieve, then stir them into the gel.

● Try using a polythene bag to dispense the gel, cutting off one corner and using it rather like an icing bag. If you find this difficult an old washing-up liquid bottle makes a good alternative. Squeeze a thin ribbon of the gel containing the seeds into the drill, and then cover with soil as normal.

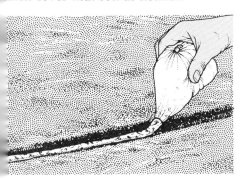

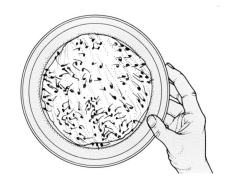

Variations You can achieve similar results by germinating the seeds indoors mixed with vermiculite or perlite, and then sprinkling the mixture into the rows when the seeds have germinated.

Coping with Difficult Seeds

The most difficult or unpredictable seeds to germinate are usually trees, shrubs, many alpines and some hardy border plants. Some may simply lose their viability quickly, but many more go into a stage of dormancy that has to be broken before they will germinate.

Most of the seeds in the categories mentioned require a period of cold – which they will receive if you leave them sown outdoors for a winter. When the warmth returns after a period of cold they are more likely to germinate. This process can be speeded up by pre-chilling the seeds in a refrigerator (1–5°C/34–41°F) before sowing. Sow them on damp kitchen paper in a covered box (otherwise the paper and seeds will dry out very rapidly in the fridge), and leave them there for about at least two weeks before sowing.

A few seeds, such as primulas and even beetroot contain a germination inhibitor that has to be removed before they will germinate well. In nature rain will eventually do this, but it can be washed out before sowing. Primula seeds can be steeped in water at 25°C (77°F) for two hours, changing the water every 10 minutes. Beetroot and New Zealand spinach can be soaked in water for 24 hours (but no longer).

Seeds Needing Special Treatment

SEEDS THAT NEED LIGHT

Ageratum
Begonia semperflorens
Bellis perennis (double daisy)
Impatiens
Lobelia
Stocks
Nicotiana
Pansy
Petunia
Phacelia campanularia
Salvia splendens

SEEDS THAT NEED DARKNESS

Eccremocarpus scaber
Nigella (love-in-a-mist)

Establishing a Framework

Colour is what usually gives a garden impact, but plants with shape and form give it structure and a sense of design. It is not how much money you spend on plants, or how many you buy, that makes a garden look well planted and well designed. It is the choice and juxtaposition that are important.

Choosing Plants

A plantsman's garden may be crammed with plants, many of them unusual or even obscure. It may be a treasure-trove of discovery for another keen plantsman, but it may not be a well-designed or properly planned garden. Unless you are really keen on collecting plants for their own sake, choose your key plants rather as you might choose furniture for the home. You would not buy a chair just because it was unusual, or even pretty, unless it matched the general decor of the room. If overall appearance and impact is your priority, plants should be chosen because they fulfil a need, fit in with the surroundings and other inhabitants, and suit the conditions that you can provide. This is especially important with woody plants that form the backbone of the garden.

Framework Plants

If you are starting a new garden from scratch, or totally redesigning an old one, you have every opportunity to give it shape and form with plants as well as

If you inherit a neglected garden, it is easy to dismiss it as having no scope. But a combination of imagination and determination can transform the most unpromising site within a relatively short time. This garden makes the most of an ordinary site.

by hard landscaping (paving and walling for instance). Even if, because of time, effort, or expense, you do not want to redesign your existing garden completely, there is still a lot that you can do to give it a new image with plants alone.

Whether starting from scratch or modifying what is there, never remove a tree or large shrub until you are absolutely sure that it cannot be incorporated into the new plan. Nothing gives a garden an impression of maturity more than trees or large shrubs, so try to retain as many as possible – at least until the replacements reach a respectable size. Do not let existing plants dictate the layout and design of your garden, however.

If you have a large shrub that you want to keep but it is in the wrong place, try moving it rather than throwing it away. You have nothing to lose if the plant would have to be destroyed anyway. Even bushy shrubs of 1.8 m (6 ft) and more can be moved successfully with a little determination and a lot of effort. Such large shrubs are difficult to dig out (and you need to retain as much soil as possible on the roots), and require lots of muscle-power to move as well as frequent watering for the first season afterwards, but they often recover.

The Overall Pattern

Before you do any planting, look at the garden critically to make sure that the 'planting blocks' are in the right place and in proportion to open areas (lawn, patio, gravel). Always go out into the garden to visualize your plans – a wall that appears relatively insignificant on a drawn plan, because it is a thin line, may assume a very different proportion when you are in the garden. Getting the proportions right of all the elements that make up the garden can make the difference between a simple collection of plants and a garden with form and pattern to it.

Although we are not dealing here in detail with garden design, there are a few basic rules that will help:

● Keep the lines and design simple – do not over-decorate it.

● Consider the garden – sitting or paved areas, lawns, flower beds and borders – as *patterns* on paper. If you start with the plants you will end up building the garden round these, instead of choosing plants to make the design work.

● Decide whether you want the garden to be inward-looking and intimate – in which case you want to keep the eye

Successful Transplanting

- If possible, start six months or a year before you move the plant. Dig a trench round the plant, about 30 cm (1 ft) out from the main stem, cutting through any thick lateral roots to encourage the plant to form new fibrous roots within the final root-ball. Return the soil to the trench.

- Water the plant *thoroughly* before moving it, if the weather is at all dry.

- Have the new planting hole excavated and ready. If the plant will benefit from pruning, do it now so that it is easier to manage.

- On the day of the move, dig a trench all round the plant, following any very thick roots farther out if necessary. Gradually work the spade beneath the plant all round the trench. There will probably be some thick roots going straight down, but you may have little option but to saw or chop through these. Make the root-ball as large as you can, bearing in mind the size of the plant and the help available.

- Place sacking or thick polythene under one side of the root-ball while it is still in the hole, roll the plant over on to it, and pull the material round the other side. By tying it round the ball of soil as firmly as possible, it is possible to avoid too much soil falling off the roots as you move the plant.

- A small plant can often be moved by one person on a wheelbarrow, a large one may require two helpers.

- Remove the sacking or polythene when the plant is positioned in its new home, and be prepared to adjust the height by excavating or adding soil.

- *Water well*, not just when you move it, but for the rest of the season, whenever the ground is dry.

- Mulch the damp soil.

- If moving an evergreen, give it temporary wind protection (hessian or polythene around a framework of canes). A transplanting spray helps.

Even with all these precautions, the plant will probably wilt, and some leaves may turn yellow or even fall. Even so, it may recover, so wait until the following spring if there are any signs of life.

Deciduous shrubs are best moved when they are dormant. Evergreens have to be moved in leaf, and spring is the ideal time.

Dividing a garden into smaller sections so that you have to explore them like the rooms of a house, will often make even a small garden more interesting. This is achieved here with a row of arches clothed in roses.

within the garden and to a large extent block out surrounding views – or whether you want to make the most of views beyond – in which case you need a more open design, taking the eye outwards. If you want to give a small garden an impression of greater size, make sure you cannot take it all in at once; even a small garden can be divided into smaller sections or have parts screened off with plants so that you have to move round the plants to see all that is there – try to avoid an open area in the middle with straight borders round the edge. An interesting design for a small garden is shown on the opposite page.

● Do not let an existing path dictate the design, otherwise it will become one of the key features with the garden designed around it.

● If you want a formal pattern, perhaps based on rectangles, do not assume that the grid has to be parallel or at right-angles to the house. Try the grid at a 45 degree angle to the house or boundary.

● Avoid lines that emphasize a problem. If the garden is long and narrow, do not have a path or bed going straight down the whole length of the garden.

● Use plants to screen unsightly objects, but remember that plants can also be used to channel the eye to a favourable aspect.

Boundaries

Start by planning the boundaries – even if you decide to have a very 'open' garden, taking advantage of attractive views beyond, you need to think about this first as it will influence how you plant the rest of the garden.

If the view beyond the garden is pleasant – whether an exceptionally good neighbouring garden or open countryside – there is a lot to be said for leading the eye beyond the boundary. If you want a hedge it can be low and informal; if you want to make it animal-proof some plastic-coated wire fencing can be unobtrusive, especially if you grow plants in front of it, or even use it as a support for climbers.

The desire for a panoramic view has to be balanced against the need for shelter. If you live in an exposed position, shelter may be particularly important. A dense shrub border, or a good collection of small trees, may provide some protection without looking too formal.

In a town garden, the problem is much more likely to be that of trying to block out a view. Bringing the focal

Don't be too rigid in your approach to boundaries. A combination of walls, fences, hedges and wall-shrubs can often be much more interesting than hedges or fences alone. Walls and fences also offer planting opportunities.

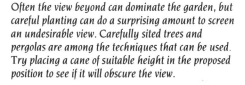

Often the view beyond can dominate the garden, but careful planting can do a surprising amount to screen an undesirable view. Carefully sited trees and pergolas are among the techniques that can be used. Try placing a cane of suitable height in the proposed position to see if it will obscure the view.

Keeping Out Noise

Besides providing shelter for the garden and privacy for its inhabitants, hedges also filter noise, and it is worth considering this aspect if you live in a noisy environment.

A single hedge on its own may be insufficient to make much impact, but by planting plenty of shrubs in front of it in as deep a bed as possible, the improvement can be significant. Evergreens will be more effective than deciduous shrubs for this purpose.

points within the garden helps to diminish the impact of the surrounding area, but sometimes you will want to block out an offending view as completely as possible.

This can often be done very successfully – if you are concerned only with the view from the garden level – by a suitable choice and positioning of trees and shrubs, or maybe a screen wall. If you are overlooked and want to create an area of privacy, think about constructing a pergola. Planted with attractive climbing plants this will give a fragrant refuge.

If you need to block out a view, do not assume that high boundary planting is necessarily the best solution. Foreground planting can be more effective because it is closer to the eye and therefore screens a wider area.

Planning on paper alone can be difficult. Enlist the help of a friend holding a long pole or cane to represent a tree or large shrub. Then take up a position with your back to the house and get your helper to move around the garden adjusting the distance of the cane away from you, until you find the position or height that provides the best screen. The closer the screening plant is to you the shorter it needs to be. Alternatively, an overhead structure may be best.

Hedge, Fence or Wall?

Placing trees and shrubs in strategic positions within the garden to enhance or obscure the view *beyond* the garden is an important part of the garden framework but it is the boundaries that can dominate the garden and set the tone for the rest of the planting. They will be the backdrop for many of the beds and borders, and unless the garden is very large you will see them from most parts of the garden. Getting them right is worth the effort.

Hedges generally provide the best form of shelter for other plants (see page 88), but you have to wait for the results and they need regular maintenance. Walls are permanent and need no regular maintenance, they make a superb background for wall shrubs and many other plants, and give a high level of privacy, if high enough. A wall need not look bare. If you do not want to plant against it, paint it a pale colour and use plants of strong shape (phormiums, yuccas, fatsias, for instance) in front.

As walls are expensive and labour-intensive to construct, fences are more popular. They are aesthetically less pleasing though: they soon look shabby unless treated with a preservative regularly, and this means that it is difficult to

Right A *cedar wood screen divides this garden in half and provides an effective background for plants.*

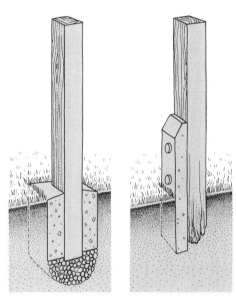

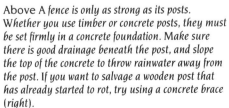

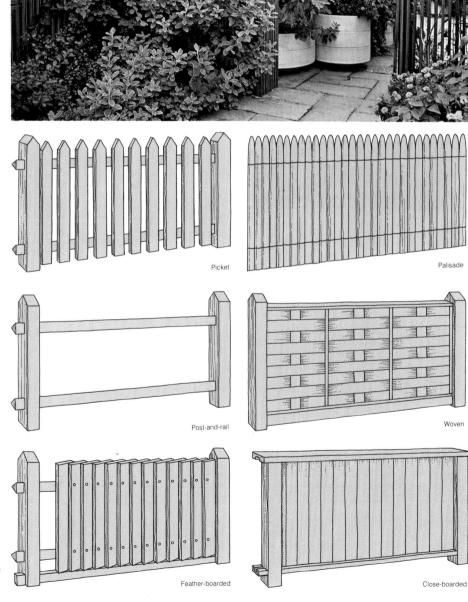

Picket

Palisade

Post-and-rail

Woven

Feather-boarded

Close-boarded

Above A *fence is only as strong as its posts. Whether you use timber or concrete posts, they must be set firmly in a concrete foundation. Make sure there is good drainage beneath the post, and slope the top of the concrete to throw rainwater away from the post. If you want to salvage a wooden post that has already started to rot, try using a concrete brace (right).*

Right *Choose a style of fencing that is in keeping with the area. For example, a painted picket fence can look superb in a cottage garden setting but may look out of place in an urban housing estate; a timber post-and-rail fence tends to imply a rural setting.*

Concrete can be used decoratively and creatively. These screen blocks make a pleasant setting for the shrubs, and act as a useful windbreak within the garden.

use perennial climbers on them. You can, however, provide a satisfactory screen of evergreen shrubs a little way in front that will still leave room for routine maintenance.

As walls and fences take no nutrients from the soil, it is easier to grow plants up to the boundary than it is with a hedge. But bear in mind that there will still be a rain shadow that makes the soil drier than in the open garden.

Do not be afraid to mix materials. A hedge planted on a low, double wall containing soil can look very effective, and will make the base more animal-proof; wall and fence combinations can also look quite attractive.

Do not overlook the use of screen walls and hedges *within* the garden. They can help to give a sense of mystery, and by dividing the garden into 'rooms' or sections may add much to the overall design. Generally internal hedges can be more informal and decorative than boundary hedges – maybe roses or lavender, a flowering berberis or spiraea.

Choosing a Hedge

There are many kinds of hedge, some of them purely decorative or used as a design feature within the garden: low box edging to formal beds, dwarf hedges of lavender or the purple-leaved *Berberis thunbergii* 'Atropurpurea Nana' are examples. The hedges described in this chapter are the more functional sort that will provide privacy and shelter for the garden.

The choice of possible hedging and screening plants is wide. Sometimes it is worth experimenting with less conventional hedges, but to be sure of an efficient windbreak for a difficult site, it is wise to choose one of the traditional plants listed below.

It is the spacing and clipping, and the plant's ability to tolerate it, that makes a good hedge. The beech grows into a huge tree if given the opportunity, but planted close and trimmed regularly, it

can provide a hedge suitable for even quite a modest garden.

There are plenty of purely decorative hedges that have the height, and impenetrability to qualify as good barriers, but some of these – roses for example – lack the year-round cover that is necessary for good garden *protection*. If you have a sheltered site, consider some of the alternatives not covered in the Table, which includes only those plants that are primarily for shelter hedges, although most of them are very decorative too.

Planting and training Hedges are among the most permanent features in the garden. You normally have only one opportunity to get the ground in good condition, so prepare it thoroughly well in advance of planting.

● Dig two spits (spade-depths) deep if the ground is poorly drained, and incorporate as much well-rotted manure or garden compost as you can spare. Level the ground then rake in a general fertilizer at about 140 g per sq m (4 oz per sq yd).

● Always firm the soil around the roots well after planting (mid to late autumn is a good time to plant deciduous hedges, mid or late spring is ideal for evergreens). If the site is very exposed, it is a good idea to erect a temporary screen or fence.

● Always water well for the first few months if the ground is dry, and try using a foliar feed for the first year; this may seem a lot of trouble to go to for a hedge, but getting the shrubs off to a good start will make a big difference, especially on a difficult site.

● Start pruning early. Cut back straggly stems, and even upward growth to level off the plants if some are taller than others, soon after planting. Do not remove the growing tips of tall conifers intend to make a *high* screen until they grow above the required height.

Some Evergreen Hedges

Name	Recommended height	Formal/informal	Main feature	Remarks
1 *Berberis* × *stenophylla*	1.8m (6ft)	informal	flowers	tolerates dry and alkaline soil
2 *Buxus sempervirens* (box)	0.3–1.2 m (1–4 ft)	formal	foliage	height depends on variety
3 *Carpinus betulus* (hornbeam)	1.5–2.4 m (5–8 ft)	formal	foliage	deciduous, but dead leaves hang all winter
4 *Cupressocyparis leylandii* (Leyland cypress)	3–4.5 m (10–15 ft)	formal	foliage	fast-growing conifer
5 *Fagus sylvatica* (beech)	1.5–2.4 m (5–8 ft)	formal	foliage	deciduous, but dead leaves hang all winter
6 *Ilex aquifolium* (holly)	1.5–1.8 m (5–6 ft)	formal	foliage	a good barrier, but avoid a draughty position
7 *Lonicera nitida* (shrubby honeysuckle)	0.6–1.4 m (2–4 ft)	formal	foliage	tolerates dry, alkaline soils. Grows in towns
8 *Prunus laurocerasus* (laurel)	1.5–1.8 m (5–6 ft)	formal	foliage	good in industrial areas
9 *Taxus baccata* (yew)	0.9–1.8 m (3–6 ft)	formal	foliage	conifer; not as slow-growing as reputed. Tolerates shade, needs good drainage

Safety

- For safety's sake, try to choose a trimmer with a lock-off switch (the locking button must be pushed in before the on-off switch can be used).

- A brightly coloured flex is more likely to be seen.

- It is always worth using a residual current device (earth-leakage circuit breaker) on all electrical garden equipment.

- Do not work in rain.

- Pass the flex over your shoulder, and preferably through a belt at the back, to keep loose flex away from the cutting blade.

- Wear thick gloves, even in summer. Most hedgetrimmer accidents involve blade injuries to the hands – thick gloves will not prevent these accidents, but they can minimize the damage.

Keeping it in trim Trimming a hedge can be tiring work, but suitable shears or trimmers will help. If there is only a small amount of hedge, hand clipping is satisfying; if the hedge is long or high, a powered hedgetrimmer is an almost essential investment. Even so, some hedges with large leaves, such as laurel, are best trimmed with secateurs otherwise the clipped leaves turn brown.

Shaping up Nothing draws unwelcome attention to a clipped hedge more than an ocean wave effect. Some gardeners have the knack of cutting a straight line; if you don't, use a string stretched along the length and trim to this.

It is beneficial to have sloping rather than vertical sides. If the hedge tapers from the base to the top, more light will reach the lower areas, and the hedge will be less likely to be damaged by a heavy fall of snow.

For ease of maintenance keep the hedge to a height that can be cut easily from the ground, but if you want privacy the hedge will inevitably be too tall to be cut without using steps of some kind. If possible use two small stepladders with a *stout*, wide plank stretched between them to work from.

Choosing shears Shears must be comfortable, and it will probably be weight and balance that will have most effect on this.

Most shears have straight-edged blades; curved or wavy blades can make cutting easier: they cut through thicker wood more readily and, unlike straight blades, tend to trap the twigs for cutting rather than pushing them out. On the negative side, they are likely to be more difficult to sharpen.

Choosing a trimmer If you have a large hedge too far from the house to make an electric hedgetrimmer a sensible option, you will probably have to consider a petrol trimmer. These are widely used by professional gardeners, but most amateurs, cutting relatively infrequently, will probably find them heavy and more difficult to use. It is worth hiring one before you buy, to see how you get on with it.

Most hedges in modern gardens are within easy cable reach of the house, and an electric hedgetrimmer is likely to be the best choice. The longer the blade, the faster you should complete the cut. You should be able to cut about twice as much with a 600 mm (2 ft) blade as with a 300 mm (1 ft) blade in the same time. A long blade will also enable you to reach higher up or across the hedge without ladders. But longer blades usually mean heavier and less easily managed machines.

Blades that cut on both sides are not necessarily better than those with teeth on only one side – some people tend to

Hedge shaping. There are many advantages to shaping the hedge with slightly tapering sides: the top may be flat, round headed or wedge shaped.

use them with a sweep in one direction only anyway. The number of teeth can make a difference. The more teeth there are, the finer the cut is likely to be; the fewer and more spaced the teeth, the larger the twigs they can tackle easily.

Renovating a hedge If there are dead sections of hedge, where the whole plant has died, there is little option but to remove the dead plants and replant with young ones. Provided the death is not due to a soil-borne disease, the hedge should gradually fill out again within a few years. But make sure you enrich the soil and feed the new plants to give them chance to compete.

If the hedge has gone bare at the base, or simply become too wide and thick, hedges that respond to hard pruning – such as yew, privet, hawthorn, and beech – can be cut back drastically into old wood. But do the job in stages: one side of the hedge one year, the other side the next, or the year after.

A common cause of hedges being poorly covered at the base is competition from weeds and other plants. Simply keeping the hedge weeded, and allowing plenty of light to the base will sometimes help.

Holes or gaps higher in the hedge can often be filled in simply by being careful not to trim too far into those areas.

Although flowering hedges need careful pruning, they can make an eyecatching feature. Here a forsythia hedge brightens up a spring day.

Framework Plants

Once you have decided on the garden boundary or considered ways of improving what you have, it is a good idea to think about trees and shrubs that have to screen a view or add height. There are many hundreds of suitable candidates, even for a small garden, but those suggested here are all widely available and generally easy to grow.

Quick-growing Trees

Both birches and eucalyptus are well worth growing in a moderately large garden. They have an attractive outline, and can give even a new garden an established look within about four or five years.

You could have an interesting garden with birches alone – most have a graceful outline, interesting peeling bark and usually a brief period of autumn colour. They are also very easy to grow – they are frequently among the first trees to colonize neglected land. Any commonly available species should do well in most gardens, but try to find a position where winter sun can fall on the bark.

For a really fast-growing tree that is evergreen into the bargain, try a eucalyptus. Many species are hardy enough to grow in southern Britain, but E. *gunnii* and E. *dalrympleana* should still survive in a cold area unless conditions are exceptionally severe. They may be damaged by a bad winter, but they usually shoot again and recover. Eucalyptus make large trees quickly, so do not choose them for a small garden.

The mountain ash or rowan, *Sorbus aucuparia*, makes a round-headed tree with pretty foliage, enhanced by orange-red berries in late summer and early autumn. There is a bonus of good autumn colour, it flowers and fruits at an early age, and it won't outgrow its welcome. Many other sorbus are also suitable.

The stag's-horn sumach, *Rhus typhina* would be worth planting even if growth were slow – it has a much-branched spreading habit, and large pinnately-divided leaves that take on brilliant red shades before they fall in autumn.

For a flowering tree that will bloom at an early age, and look respectable within a few years, the laburnums are worth considering. Try 'Vossii' – it has long chains of yellow flowers and sets few of the poisonous seeds.

Trees for Shape

No matter how attractive the individual trees, if you choose only species and varieties with a normal round-headed shape, they can become boring for most of the year. Try to include a few trees with a distinctive outline.

Even a small group of trees and shrubs can give a garden height and structure, especially if they have contrasting colours and shapes. In this group there is a purple-leaved Prunus cerasifera 'Pissardii', golden Philadelphus coronarius 'Aureus', a spiky yucca, and the fastigiate (upright) Prunus 'Amanogawa'.

Contorted trees are most effective planted where you can view their winter outline against the skyline. Two that are easy to grow and particularly striking are *Salix matsudana* 'Tortuosa' and *Corylus avellana* 'Contorta'.

Fastigiate trees, which have a narrow, upright habit, can look rather stark on their own, but as part of a mixed group they often add interest. They are particularly useful in a small garden, or even a large one where you want to give height without casting too much shade. There are fastigiate forms of many common trees, but worth looking out for are *Carpinus betulus* 'Columnaris', *Malus tschonoskii*, and *Prunus* 'Amanogawa'. The malus does not have such attractive flowers and fruit as most flowering crab apples, but it has magnificent autumn colour. The prunus is an attractive flowering tree.

Focal Point Trees

You may have decided to include a slower-growing but eye-catching tree to act as a focal point or to grow as a specimen in a lawn. Many of the trees already mentioned could be used, but there are other small or medium-sized flowering trees that will add more colour to the height.

Two families of flowering trees – *Malus* and *Prunus* – are so important that it is very difficult to limit the choice to just a few.

For flower power among the flowering crabs, choose *Malus floribunda*, which makes a small, round-headed tree covered with pale pink flowers, crimson in bud, at the end of April. 'John Downie' is one of the best fruiting crabs, with large, conical, orange and red fruit (they can be used in preserves). It has pink-budded white flowers in late May. 'Golden Hornet' has small yellow fruits, but there are masses of them, and they can last for months. It is also a good pollinator if you have ordinary apple trees in the garden. If you prefer a tree with reddish foliage, try 'Profusion' which has coppery crimson young foliage, maturing to a more bronzy-green. The red flowers are followed by deep red fruit.

The *Prunus* family includes the Japanese cherries, and the almond (P. *dulcis*), which is one of the earliest trees to flower in spring. For size of flower and depth of colour, however, the Japanese cherries are the ones to choose. One of the most commonly planted is 'Kanzan', a strong-growing medium-sized tree with stiffly erect branches when young.

Trees for shape. Many trees have distinctive outlines which add to their effectiveness as framework plants. Three of the most usual are shown here: the round headed, fastigiate and weeping.

The large double flowers are a showy pink. There are many equally good varieties including P. × *yedoensis*, which has a profusion of double pink turning to white flowers in mid-spring.

It is always worth trying to include multi-merit trees for a focal point position, and the shad bush or snowy mespilus, A*melanchier lamarckii*, is one of these. It may be sold as A. *canadensis* (a separate but very similar species), but it does not really matter which one you buy – both become a mass of white in spring, and take on a new emphasis in autumn when the leaves turn to rich orange-reds. The snowy mespilus is more commonly grown as a bushy shrub, so if you want it as a tree make sure you buy one suitably trained.

Most gardeners associate the *Cornus* family with the dogwoods that have coloured winter stems, but it also contains some of the most 'architecturally' beautiful trees that will add considerably to the shape and texture of the garden as well as giving it height.

Cornus controversa 'Variegata' has wide, spreading branches in tiers. It is worth growing for shape alone, but it also has prettily variegated creamy-white and green narrow leaves. Unfortunately it is slow-growing. C. *kousa* also has spreading tiered branches, but is much more spectacular in flower, when the branches are covered with large, star-like white bracts in late spring or early summer. Strawberry-like fruits are sometimes produced, but in Britain these are something of a bonus and should not be relied upon. You can usually depend on good autumn colour.

Weeping Trees

Just as fastigiate trees are useful for introducing a change of shape and outline to the garden framework, so do weeping trees. Unlike fastigiate trees, however, they are best planted as isolated specimens where their shape can be appreciated and where their symmetry will not be spoilt.

If you have space for only one weeping tree, it is probably best to choose one with attractive flowers or fruits. One that is small enough for even a tiny garden is *Cotoneaster* 'Hybridus Pendulus'. The white flowers are not spectacular, but the plant comes into its own when the masses of bright red berries light up the cascading branches in autumn. The plant is normally a low carpeter, but it can be grafted onto an erect stem, so if you order by post, make sure you are buying a standard form, and not a ground-cover plant.

If there really are space constraints, consider *Caragana arborescens* 'Pendula'; this is not a spectacular plant but it is tough and compact, and has pretty leaves and yellow pea-type flowers.

Weeping cherries are always popular and perhaps the best is *Prunus* 'Kiku-shidare Sakura', with its cascading branches studded with pink pom-pom double flowers.

Worth growing for shape alone is the graceful weeping birch, *Betula pendula*

Multi-merit trees are always worth planting. Cornus kousa chinensis *is one of these. It has an attractive, almost pagoda-like shape, masses of very long-lasting flowers, often good autumn colour, and sometimes the bonus of decorative red fruits that resemble strawberries in appearance.*

'Youngii', which is an ideal tree to provide a little shade in a small garden. If you prefer a small weeping tree with coloured foliage, the weeping purple beech, F*agus sylvatica* 'Purpurea Pendula' will make a small, mushroom-headed tree. Do not be deterred by the fact that it is a beech; this one is suitable for a small garden. Justifiably the most popular silver-leaved weeping tree is the weeping willow-leaved pear, *Pyrus salicifolia* 'Pendula'. It makes a silvery mound, and although they are not a feature from a distance, there are white flowers in mid-spring and small brownish fruits in autumn.

Most weeping willows become alarmingly large trees, but there are some more modest ones such as the Kilmarnock willow, *Salix caprea* 'Pendula'. This makes a small umbrella-like tree with attractive catkins in spring.

Trees for Colour and Texture
In the search for trees with a good outline or pretty flowers, do not overlook those with coloured leaves or green but distinctive leaves that will be a feature in their own right. These will often contribute much more to the garden than the more brilliant but fleeting displays of flowering trees.

There are lots of superb maples, but for spring colour A*cer pseudoplatanus* 'Brilliantissimum' is one of the finest – the young leaves are shrimp-pink, then pale bronze. Unfortunately they gradually mature to an uninspiring green. For autumn colour, A. *japonicum* 'Vitifolium' is one of the best.

If you can provide a sheltered site, *Aralia elata*, the angelica tree, makes a good small tree for foliage effect. It has angelica-like leaves up to 1 m (3 ft) long. The feathery white flower heads in late summer are a bonus. Be prepared to remove any suckers.

Catalpas can grow into large trees, but the kinds with purple-flushed or yellow leaves are usually smaller. *Catalpa bignonioides* 'Aurea' makes a superb

tree with its large yellow foliage; C. × *erubescens* 'Purpurea' is less spectacular, but it has a nice spreading habit and the young shoots have dark purple-black leaves before they mature to dark green. Both need a sheltered position to do well and to avoid the large leaves being damaged by strong winds.

One form of the honey locust, *Gleditsia triacanthos* 'Sunburst', is another foliage tree to consider. It will make a medium-sized tree, but the young feathery foliage is bright yellow.

Robinia pseudoacacia 'Frisia' is similar, and now widely planted. It can have a suckering, shrubby habit, but if trained properly it makes a small to medium-sized tree with feathery-looking yellow foliage that does not fade.

Catalpa bignonioides 'Aurea', *a superb tree for adding colour and 'texture' to the garden, but it needs a protected position to do well.*

Using Conifers
Invaluable though conifers are, they need very careful placing. Most of them have a neat, columnar or oval outline that can be useful where you want a clean-cut, almost formal appearance, perhaps to frame a garden view, rather like pillars. As screens and hedges, or as a background for other plants, they can be superb. But it is easy to have too many upright conifers that do not fit in with a natural and flowing garden design. Frequently they grow too large, and can dominate the garden.

It is usually safe to use dwarf conifers freely in the rock garden, or among plants that associate well with them, such as heathers, and benefit from the height and colour contrast provided, but taller-growing conifers should be chosen and placed with restraint. Unless the garden is large, choose just a few specimen trees and make a real feature of them.

For most modern gardens, a tree that does not exceed 10 m (30 ft) in 25 years would be suitable. The monkey puzzle tree (*Araucaria araucana*) qualifies, although it will eventually grow much larger. A good golden Lawson cypress is *Chamaecyparis lawsoniana* 'Lane' (syn. 'Lanei'), but it needs a sunny position to look its best.

If you simply want an upright or columnar conifer to give vertical emphasis to part of the garden, choose one such as *Chamaecyparis lawsoniana* 'Ellwoodii' (grey foliage, about 3 m [26 ft] after 25 years), or *Juniperus scopulorum* 'Skyrocket' (grey foliage, about 7 m [24 ft] after 25 years).

Some dwarf and prostrate conifers are listed on page 113.

Architectural Plants

Trees, more than any other plant, give a garden its framework, and the third dimension – height. But strong shapes and outlines are useful among the lower planting levels too. Even a few isolated plants with a strong 'architectural' outline can give your garden a touch of distinction.

For a 'tropical' effect, try *Cordyline australis*, a palm-like tree that will grow slowly to 6 m (20 ft) or more in favourable areas. Young plants can be kept in tubs and given protection in cold districts, but large specimens in the ground are only likely to survive in favourable southern parts of Britain. The Chusan or fan palm will grow in northern areas if there is a very favourable local climate, otherwise this is another one for southern Britain. It can reach 9 m (30 ft) or so, but it is only likely to reach this size in warm districts. Both these plants need very careful placing – they are superb in the right setting, say in a gravelled garden perhaps in association with other distinctive plants such as phormiums and yuccas.

Bamboos seem to fit in whatever the style of garden, from the true Japanese garden to an ordinary backyard garden where they perhaps screen the garage. But there are lots of them, some dwarf, others large and rampant; some quite tender, others tough and hardy.

Phormiums (New Zealand flax) are particularly striking, and again there are many kinds, from tall ones 2–3 m (6–10 ft) tall to dwarfs of about 60 cm (2 ft) or less, from the plain green to those with red, purple, and cream variegations. All have the same distinctive spiky appearance with clumps of broad sword-like leaves (the tips of those varieties derived from P. *cookianum* are drooping). They should be hardy in all parts of Britain, *once established*, though in very severe areas or winters they may be cut back or even killed.

A group of conifers with contrasting shapes and colours makes a successful garden feature and provides year-round interest.

Yuccas (Y. *filamentosa* and Y. *gloriosa*) have spiky rosettes of evergreen strap-like leaves and truly imposing spikes of massive white bell flowers. Use yuccas to provide a focal point, or in say a gravel garden, rather than trying to mix them among more conventional shrubs.

The false castor oil plant, *Fatsia japonica*, with large, glossy, evergreen hand-like leaves and ball-like heads of white flowers late in the year can make a really distinctive feature. It can easily make a shrub 1.8 m (6 ft) or more high and wide, and it ought to be given space to be appreciated.

Striking Herbaceous Plants

As well as these woody plants there are many herbaceous plants with a distinctive shape or form, and these should be used also to create a distinctive atmosphere. Try plants such as *Gunnera manicata*, like a giant rhubarb with leaves perhaps 1.5 m/5 ft across, it needs waterside conditions, red-hot pokers (*Kniphofia* species and varieties), *Miscanthus sacchariflorus*, an ornamental grass forming a clump of up to 3 m (10 ft) high, and the ornamental rhubarb *Rheum palmatum*, with huge leaves and reddish flowers to 1.8 m (6 ft.).

Phormiums have a strong outline that makes them striking feature plants. They are hardy in most parts of Britain once established, and there are now many fine varieties with coloured or variegated foliage.

Filling in the Detail

You may prefer the subtle effect of foliage or the more muted colours of many cottage-garden plants to the almost garish vivid colours of some modern annuals or highly bred plants such as dahlias or tulips, but how you mix and use colours and arrange the plants will set the tone and style of your garden.

Planning for Colour

The colour wheel shows which colours will harmonize and which will contrast, but no matter how much time you spend planning colour schemes for individual flowers or border combinations, the results are likely to be disappointing if you concentrate on flower colour alone. With the exception of some plants, the flowering period of individual border plants is often quite brief, and two plants that may flower at the same time one year may not overlap so well another time. Always try to consider flower colour in relation to the background (green hedge or lawn, patio walling, or other plants) and to the foliage of surrounding plants. Combinations of flowers and foliage can often be far more striking and dependable than combinations of flower colours alone.

Foliage colours need not be boring – there are lots of silvers, greys, and yellows, and variegated plants, as well as almost every conceivable shade of green. Leaves that open pale green, or even yellow, may age to dark green, and autumn brings its own tapestry of rich colours. Avoid being so rigid in colour

Trees and shrubs form the backbone of a garden, but herbaceous and ground-cover plants give it form and texture. Try to keep a balance between them.

planning that you miss the beauty of those plants that reflect the changing seasons.

Colours can affect the way a garden is perceived. They can make a bed or border seem larger or smaller than it really is. Hot colours (see colour wheel) tend to attract attention, so they are best placed towards the front of a border. Bold red or yellow plants placed at the end of the garden may make it seem shorter or smaller by their dominance. Cool colours make good foils and are often useful placed behind the warmer colours; they have the effect of making a garden seem longer.

Colour Wheel

The six basic colours or hues are shown here, together with their adjacent colours. Red, orange and yellow are 'hot' colours; violet, blue and green are 'cool' colours. Adding grey

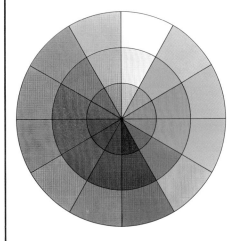

to a hue produces a tone of that colour which is darker, adding white produces a tint which is lighter. As a rule you can safely assume that colours on opposite sides of the wheel will go together even though they are very different and striking. These are called complementary colours and they can work very well together to give a bold effect, but they can also sometimes look too strident. The closer colours are together on the wheel, the more they will harmonize. Both harmonies and contrasts are useful, but contrasts are often more acceptable if an intermediate colour on the wheel is used too (green foliage often has this effect anyway). If you are looking for harmonies, go for tones or tints rather than the pure colours.

How We See Colour

Light from the sun arrives as a mixture of different wavelengths (the component parts can be seen when the water droplets in a rainbow reflect and refract sunlight). Colour is also produced when the light falls on anything that absorbs some wavelengths and reflects others: this is how we perceive most plant colours.

The plant contains pigments, which are not in themselves coloured but have the ability to absorb colours (wavelengths) selectively. A 'blue' pigment looks blue because it absorbs all colours except blue – which it reflects.

Reds These can be difficult to handle. While two shades of yellow or two blues can usually be relied upon to go well together, two reds can jar horribly. It is best to keep different shades of red well separated. If you try to use red or pinks for a 'theme' bed the results are likely to be disappointing. Pinks and reds do associate well with silver, and there are plenty of silver-leaved border and bedding plants.

Green and gold Green is everywhere in the garden, so it is easy to take it for granted. If you are looking for year-round interest, however, the many shades of evergreens come into their own – and golden and variegated kinds are particularly useful. Conifers are especially good for foliage effect, since they come in 'blues' and golds, as well as many shades of green.

Whites If you have a garden large enough to use single colour themes, a white bed or border can be very effective. If this is not possible, use white flowers or silvery foliage to break up the bolder colours in a mixed border. Above all, regard white as a positive colour.

Silver and white plants can be surprisingly effective, alone or with other colours such as blues. Here the white-flowered Lavatera 'Mont Blanc' *has silver-leaved* Cineraria maritima 'Diamond' (left) *and* Pyrethrum ptarmicaeflorum (right) *at the base.*

Blues Wonderful for blending with most other colours, and together with grey-foliaged plants can make useful 'theme' beds.

Beauty in Bark
Barks and coloured stems are frequently overlooked, yet they make a useful contribution – to winter colour especially.

A single specimen tree placed where it can catch the winter sunshine can be a really colourful feature. There are many to choose from, including the white paperbark birch (*Betula papyrifera*), mahogany-coloured *Prunus serrula*, and cinnamon-red *Arbutus × andrachnoides*.

There are shrubs with stems that will be a feature all winter, especially some of the dogwoods such as the red-stemmed *Cornus alba* 'Sibirica' and yellow-green *C. stolonifera* 'Flaviramea'. The large arching white stems of *Rubus cockburnianus* can also light up an area of the garden when winter sunlight strikes them.

Theme Borders
If space is limited, you will almost certainly want borders with mixed colours and mixed planting (shrubs as well as herbaceous perennials), but in a large garden it is sometimes possible to devote a bed to a particular colour scheme – perhaps white and greys, though it may be necessary to introduce a few plants with blue flowers or blue-tinged foliage, or a touch of pink or yellow. Harmonies of soft blues and pinks, and perhaps cream, is another possibility. The success of this type of bed requires a good knowledge of plants and dash of artistic talent.

'Rainbow borders' use a progression of colours along the border, starting with, say, white or yellow and working through to reds at the other end (or the centre if the border is long enough). Because flowering times vary so much the graduated effect is more often theoretical than practical, but at least

With a careful choice of plants, borders can be made interesting over a long period. Here late summer is still colourful with late-flowering kniphofias, border chrysanthemums, Michaelmas daisies, Japanese anemones and salvia.

you should not have any clashes provided you can sort out the reds and pinks satisfactorily.

A variation on this theme can be used to give a sense of greater distance. Use strong colours such as reds and oranges at the near end, and weaker colours such as blues, mauves, and pinks towards the far end.

Mixed Borders
Some of the finest herbaceous and shrub borders appear to have colours randomly distributed. The chances are they were carefully planned. By planting in large clumps (at least three plants of each kind), the border will have large blocks of colour and the effect is usually more pleasing; even so, draw a plan on

paper first and colour in the areas with pencils or felt-tipped pens of similar colour to the flowers. Make one plan for each of the summer months, and colour in only the plants in flower at that time. This will give a good idea of potential clashes beforehand, and if you are planting in bold drifts it should not be a tiresome chore. If you find you need to avoid a clash between drifts of colour, try planting a group of white-flowered or grey-leaved plants.

Summer Bedding
The permutations of summer bedding plants and the colour schemes that can be created are limited only by your imagination. One of the advantages of seasonal bedding is that you can try out

a different colour scheme every year. But there are some 'rules' that will help to increase the chances of a successful combination.

Do not use too many different kinds of plants or colours in the same bed. If you use mixed colour varieties, keep to one or two kinds of plants (plus perhaps an edging and dot plants). Even if using separate colours, avoid too many different types – bold but simple splashes of colour are almost always more effective. Do not give several beds in close proximity totally different colour schemes. Change the plants or the planting patterns, but keep to broadly the same colours.

Do use plenty of foliage plants, not only for their longer period of interest, but also for contrast of colour and texture. Silver-leaved plants harmonize well and enhance most brightly-coloured bedding plants.

Bear in mind that colour contrasts do not always make the best bedding. Colour harmonies such as blues, purples and mauves, or yellows, oranges and bronze, can be restful and pretty.

Colours to Attract Insects

Flowers are coloured for a practical purpose – often to attract pollinating insects. Insects are attracted to bright colours from a considerable distance, though they may, of course, be guided by scent too.

The colours may not appear the same to insects as they do to us. A bee, for example, cannot see pure red but it can distinguish yellow, blue-violet and white, although it sees the last as blue-green (white light without the red element).

Variegated Plants

These are plants with white, cream or other coloured markings on the foliage. Most of them would probably be at a disadvantage in nature, because the areas of leaf that are without the green chlorophyll are less efficient at photosynthesis (see page 55) and so the plant is likely to be less vigorous. Variegated plants have a tendency to revert to the plain green forms from which they are derived. To gardeners they are attractive and most of them make good garden plants.

Variegation can be due to various factors. The silvery markings on the houseplant *Pilea cadierei* (aluminium plant) and the spots on some begonias, are caused by air blisters under the outer layer of cells.

Some variegation is due to either the outer or the inner layer of leaf tissue having defective chloroplasts. Depending on the relative thickness of the outer layer of cells, either the green cells, or the white ones (which have defective chloroplasts), give that part of the leaf its colour.

In plants with vertical stripes (in some grasses, for instance), the variegation may be due to defective chloroplasts throughout that section of leaf.

Variegation can also be caused by viruses (it is in effect a symptom of disease), but where such plants are cultivated the virus does not severely affect plant growth. Some variegated abutilons owe their attraction to the effect of a virus infection.

Arranging Plants

There are designers who manage to achieve eye-catching gardens with the minimum of plants, but what plants are used are well chosen. Most of us want to fill the garden with as many plants as possible, and unfortunately it is often this collector's instinct in us that can mar the result. A broad sweep made up of, say, three heather varieties is likely to have far more impact than growing 30 varieties in the same area. A herbaceous border composed of 10 groups each

PLANTING PLAN		
1 *Pyracantha coccinea*	23 *Rhododendron* 'Blue Diamond'	44 *Iris pumila*
2 *Rosa* 'Anna Wheatcroft'	24 *Rhododendron* 'Praecox'	45 *Bergenia cordifolia*
3 *Chamaecyparis*	25 *Hebe* 'Autumn Glory'	46 *Chamaecyparis pisifera*
4 *Rhododendron japonicum*	26 *Cytisus praecox*	47 *Chamaecyparis lawsoniana* 'Fletcheri'
5 *Erica cinerea* 'Lavender Lady'	27 *Cotinus coggygria*	48 *Smilacina racemosa*
6 *Filipendula ulmaria* 'Aurea'	28 *Iris germanica*	49 *Hebe x franciscana* 'Variegata'
7 *Ligularia clivorum* 'Desdemona'	29 *Senecio greyi*	50 *Rhododendron impeditum*
8 *Hosta* 'Frances Williams'	30 *Rhododendron* 'Vanessa'	51 *Chamaecyparis obtusa*
9 *Solidago* 'Lenmore'	31 *Betula papyrifera*	52 *Daphne collina*
10 *Astilbe* 'Fanal'	32 *Crataegus oxyacanthoides*	53 *Rhododendron* 'Elizabeth'
11 *Euphorbia polychroma*	33 *Polyanthus*	54 *Chamaecyparis lawsoniana* 'Columnaris'
12 *Juniperus sabina tamariscifolia*	34 *Prunus cerasifera* 'Nigra'	55 *Dryas octopetala*
13 *Bergenia cordifolia*	35 *Cotoneaster horizontalis*	56 *Picea glauca*
14 *Rosa* 'Evelyn Fison'	36 *Rhus typhina*	57 *Saponaria ocymoides*
15 *Potentilla fruticosa*	37 *Pinus mugo pumilio*	58 *Lonicera nitida*
16 *Cytisus scoparius*	38 *Taxus baccata* 'Fastigiata'	59 *Skimmia japonica*
17 *Viburnum carlesii*	39 *Genista hispanica*	60 *Primula juliae* 'Wanda'
18 *Cytisus scoparius*	40 *Geranium subcaulescens*	61 *Corylopsis pauciflora*
19 *Hebe* 'Pagei'	41 *Calluna vulgaris* 'Mrs Ronald Gray'	
20 *Rhododendron fastigiatum*	42 *Juniperus chinensis* 'Pfitzerana Aurea'	
21 *Fritillaria imperialis*	43 *Calluna vulgaris* 'Alba Plena'	
22 *Erica x darleyensis*		

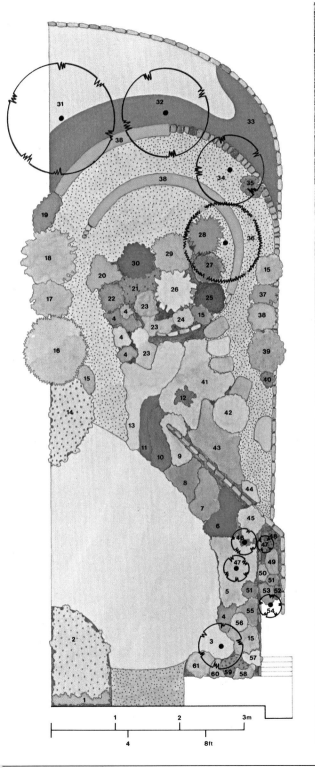

Above *Some herbaceous plants bring a last fling of autumn glory before they die down – this is* Smilacina racemosa, *with the evergreen* Hebe × franciscana *'Variegata' by its side.*

Left *A striking group of border plants, including the almost purple-leaved, yellow-flowered* Ligularia clivorum *'Desdemona', a group of bold-leaved hostas with the bonus of flowers, and one of the modern varieties of yellow golden rod* (solidago) *behind.*

Both these plant groups are incorporated in the planting plan.

containing three plants will almost certainly look more impressive than a border of 30 different individual plants. And the same principle applies even in a small garden.

This chapter is intended to show how to use plants creatively, how to get the best impact from the various types, and which plants are suitable for particular situations. Bear in mind that the plants mentioned are only *examples* of what you could use – it would be possible to write a complete book about each of the plant groups mentioned here – but in general plants that are widely available have been chosen. Always be prepared to modify plans and advice to suit your own garden. The border in a plan or picture in one book may be on different soil, have a different aspect, or be in a different part of the country. If

you have an alkaline soil, there is little point in trying to grow a plant that needs acid soil. It is better to choose an alternative. If experience shows that some plants do much better than others in your garden, concentrate on those that do well and be prepared to abandon those that do not. It may seem drastic, but it will be a lot less time consuming and frustrating than trying to coax 'poor doers'.

Instant results and long-term plans are often in conflict. But you can overcome this by the use of fast-growing plants or gap-fillers that are discarded later. If all the shrubs are planted at their final spacing, the garden is going to look very sparse for several years. If you plant extra ones between, especially some of the quick-growing shrubs listed opposite, and discard

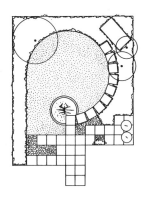

The smaller the garden, the more difficult it is to integrate the 'utilities' such as refuse bins, clothes lines, and garden sheds, without these intruding. Although small gardens like this one are a challenge, it is possible to achieve plenty of impact and a sense of design with relatively few features and without having to spend a fortune on plants.

In a small garden like this, every part must work, and even the small paved area has been broken up with inset pebbles to bring interest and a change of texture to what could otherwise be a rather plain feature.

them when they become overcrowded, you will be able to combine long-term aims with an attractive result in the short-term too.

Using Shrubs

If you have the space, shrub borders can be both attractive and fairly labour-saving. Apart from weed control (easy with chemicals if you do not want to use mulches or ground cover), and annual pruning (unlikely to be necessary with all of them), practically no maintenance will be required. The drawbacks are that in traditional shrub borders, the plants can become large, and in the competition for light often one-sided or uneven in appearance.

Another possibility is that of using shrubs in island beds in the lawn. If the beds are reasonably small, all the plants should grow well, and it will help to break up a large area of grass and make it more interesting (with less to mow).

A more open approach to planting, perhaps with generous bays for herbaceous plants or low-growing evergreens is worth considering. In a small garden especially, it is worth considering mixed borders, where suitable shrubs are used among herbaceous plants. The shrubs often have a better shape, and in winter the border looks less bleak than it would with the herbaceous plants alone.

A choice shrub, such as a shrubby magnolia, a camellia, pieris, amelanchier, kalmia, H*ibiscus syriacus*, or a yucca, makes a good specimen plant on its own in the lawn. Many viburnums can also be used successfully in this way.

Planning the Border

It is tempting to make a list of your favourite plants, then try to incorporate these into an overall plan for the bed or border. Sensible though the idea sounds, the results are likely to be disappointing. The plants need to be considered as a group, and how they

SHRUBS FOR SHADE
Aucuba japonica and varieties
Buxus sempervirens and varieties (box)
Camellia
Choisya ternata
Euonymus fortunei radicans 'Variegata'
Fatsia japonica
Hedera species and varieties*
Hypericum calycinum
Ilex (holly)*
Mahonia*
Osmanthus delavayi
Pachysandra terminalis ('Variegata' is pretty)*
Prunus laurocerasus 'Otto Luyken'*
Rhododendron
*Ruscus aculeatus**
Sarcococca
Skimmia japonica and varieties
Vinca*

If you want a plant to grow in full shade beneath deciduous trees, choose one marked with an asterisk (*)

QUICK-GROWING SHRUBS
Aucuba japonica varieties
Berberis thunbergii and varieties
Buddleia davidii
Caryopteris × *clandonensis*
Ceratostigma willmottianum
Choisya ternata
Cornus alba 'Sibirica'
Cornus stolonifera 'Flaviramea'
Cotoneaster 'Cornubia'
Cotoneaster watereri
Cytisus × *kewensis*
Cytisus scoparius
Elaeagnus × *ebbingei*
Erica carnea
Forsythia intermedia 'Spectabilis'
Fuchsia (hardy types)
Genista hispanica
Hebe 'Midsummer Beauty'
Helianthemum nummularium varieties
Hypericum calycinum
Hypericum 'Hidcote'
Kolkwitzia amabilis 'Pink Cloud'
Leycesteria formosa
Ligustrum ovalifolium 'Aureum'
Lupinus arboreus
Philadelphus coronarius
Philadelphus 'Virginal'
Potentilla fruticosa varieties
Sambucus racemosa 'Plumosa Aurea'
Senecio 'Sunshine'
Spiraea × *bumalda* 'Anthony Waterer'
Spiraea × *vanhouttei*
Viburnum tinus
Weigela garden hybrids

The evergreen Mahonica japonica, *with its scented winter flowers, will bring colour to a shady area during the most difficult season.*

Although grasses can look untidy in winter, they can make a spectacular summer feature. Here a pampas grass (Cortaderia selloana) *and* Miscanthus sinensis *make a striking display.*

relate with their neighbours, rather than as isolated plants. You should always ask yourself whether a plant fits into the overall scheme. If not, leave it out or grow it elsewhere. Choose instead one that fits the bill.

● Bear in mind, too, the size and proportion of the plants in relation to the dimension of the bed or border. It is a good idea not to plant anything that will grow taller than the widest part of the bed.

● Avoid arranging the plants in regimented rows of decreasing height – use a few taller plants among the low ones to break the regimented appearance.

● Aim for contrasting foliage colours and habits, lax spreading, bushy plants near stiff upright ones, small-leaved plants against large-leaved ones, grey foliage against green, gold, or purple.

● Tempting though it is to plant mainly evergreens, too many can make the garden predictable. Use plenty of evergreens, but mix in deciduous shrubs to provide a changing scene.

Using Border Perennials

The traditional single-sided, long herbaceous border is almost a thing of the past except in relatively few large gardens. Modern homes have smaller gardens, and there are many conflicting demands on leisure time. Traditional borders demand space and time.

If you have room for a herbaceous border, it will almost certainly be one of the features of summer. It does not have to be a single-sided border with the tallest plants at the back; an island bed with tall plants in the centre can be more effective, especially set into a large lawn. It will be more interesting if it is, say, kidney-shaped rather than a simple rectangle.

If you do not have space for herbaceous borders, there are still plenty of opportunities for using border perennials. Some of them can be used as ground cover (see page 110), or in containers (page 117), but there are also opportunities for growing them in all kinds of places around the garden if you choose suitable plants for the position. Hostas can be grown in a narrow border against a low wall or fence (though they do not like a dry position), irises can be grown in bays in a shrub border, many others can be used in a mixed border, and even individual plants with a strong outline can be used as a temporary focal point – a single plant of *Acanthus spinosus* can make an imposing feature during the summer.

When planning an herbaceous border, do not overlook the importance of foliage effect. Foliage plants, such as hostas and some ornamental grasses, will have a much longer season of interest than those grown mainly for their flowers. Try to incorporate some bold non-herbaceous plants that still look in keeping with the traditional border – pampas grass (*Cortaderia selloana* 'Pumila' is a good compact one), and phormiums for example. These 'backbone' plants will remain features while the other plants are not at their best.

Consider too the role of evergreen and winter-interest border plants (see right). A border of these alone might become boring, but by using them among those that die down in winter, you should be able to retain pockets of interest all through the year.

No matter how well you plan a border of herbaceous perennials, there will be times when the border can look drab, and even in summer there may be gaps that could usefully be filled in. Add bulbs for spring interest; even though they may not flower until early spring, the shoots usually start to emerge in mid or late winter, and this at least gives an impression of growth and activity. Autumn-flowering bulbs will also help to extend the season – try the autumn crocuses (*Colchicum* spp) and *Sternbergia lutea* (which looks like a yellow crocus and flowers in early and late autumn). To fill summer gaps, use hardy annuals or bedding plants. This technique is especially useful for a newly planted border.

they extend the season of interest and still provide ground-cover rather than bare soil.

Do not overlook the role of other evergreens that go well with border plants, such as pampas grass and phormiums. Suitable shrubs, such as rosemary, will also provide year-round interest.

WINTER INTEREST
Bergenia species and varieties
Dianthus
Epimedium
Euphorbia myrsinites
Euphorbia robbiae
Helleborus lividus corsicus (syn. *H. corsicus*)*
*Helleborus niger**
Heuchera sanguinea
Iris foetidissima
*Iris unguicularis**
Lamium galeobdolon 'Variegatum'
Lamium maculatum
Liriope muscari
Polygonum vacciniifolium
Saxifraga umbrosa (S. × *urbium* is similar)
Stachys lanata (syn. *S. byzantina*)
Tiarella cordifolia
Tolmiea menziesii
* winter-flowering

For a fast ground-cover plant with interesting foliage and flowers from late spring to mid-summer, choose one of the dead nettles, such as Lamium maculatum *illustrated here. It has an invasive habit and will colonise poor ground.*

BORDER PLANTS FOR SHADE	
Ajuga reptans	Hosta
Alchemilla mollis	Iris foetidissima
Anemone × hybrida	Lamium maculatum
Athyrium filix-femina	Matteuccia
Bergenia	struthiopteris
Brunnera macrophylla	Omphalodes
Cimicifuga racemosa	cappadocica
Convallaria majalis	Polygonatum ×
Dicentra spectabilis	hybridum
Dryopteris filix-mas	Pulmonaria
Euphorbia robbiae	angustifolia
Euphorbia wulfenii	Rodgersia pinnata
Epimedium	Tellima grandiflora
Helleborus	Tiarella cordifolia
Hemerocallis	Trillium grandiflorum

Evergreen Border Plants

Most of these plants will remain evergreen in most areas in most winters, but some of them (*Stachys lanata* for instance) may look bedraggled by the end of winter until the new leaves grow. They are, however, worth including as

Alliums are among the most spectacular of bulbous flowers and are set off to good effect here beneath a canopy of laburnum and wisteria.

Bulbs for the Border

If you search plant catalogues and the border plant sections of garden centres for inspiration, you will probably miss some of the most striking border plants. Bulbs such as lilies, summer hyacinths (*Galtonia candicans*), and the huge *Allium giganteum* are usually sold as dry bulbs.

The list below includes some of the most useful bulbs for the border, but a specialist catalogue will have many more.

Allium christophii (syn. A. *albopilosum*)
Allium giganteum
Allium karataviense
Amaryllis belladonna (do not confuse this one with the indoor 'amaryllis' – which is a hippeastrum). Only suitable for mild districts
Canna hybrids
Crocosmia
Eucomis bicolor
Galtonia candicans
Gladiolus
Iris (English, Dutch, Spanish bulbous types)
Lilium candidum
Lilium henryi
Lilium Mid Century hybrids (such as 'Enchantment')
Lilium regale
Lilium tigrinum
Tigridia pavonia

Climbers and Wall Shrubs

Climbers and wall shrubs are especially valuable in a small garden, where there are lots of walls and boundaries in relation to open planting area. They not only help to soften and hide walls and fences, they also make use of vertical space which would not otherwise be fully exploited.

Annual climbers such as sweet peas and the canary creeper (*Tropaeolum peregrinum*, syn. T. *canariensis*) are pretty, but they add nothing to the permanent structure of the garden, and as screens they are of limited use because they are effective only for a relatively short period of the year. If you want a quick annual climber for screening, try the ornamental hop, *Humulus japonicus* (there is also a variegated form, which is less vigorous but more attractive).

To clothe a wall or fence, it is best to plant mainly evergreens, with some deciduous climbers and wall shrubs that have particularly good flowers or fruit.

Wall shrubs are useful for growing against a fence or low wall, as they generally need no special support. Self-clinging climbers, such as ivies, Virginia creeper (*Parthenocissus quinquefolia*), and Boston ivy (*Parthenocissus tricuspidata*) are useful, but are generally more suitable for a large wall.

Most wall shrubs can be grown perfectly satisfactorily as free-standing plants: they simply look good trained against a wall (pyracanthas for instance). Others are often grown close to a wall primarily for the protection that the wall offers in winter (*Garrya elliptica* falls into this category).

Do not worry about climbers such as ivies harming the brickwork. Provided the pointing is in good condition they will do no harm; if the mortar is already crumbling then they could make matters worse.

Most climbers are planted against walls or fences, but they can be used more creatively too. Clematis can be grown through trees (they look superb intertwined with say laburnum or lilacs in flower at the same time); they can also be used to disguise old tree stumps. Vigorous climbing roses will climb into trees such as flowering cherries, and the mile-a-minute vine (*Polygonum baldschuanicum*) will completely hide an ugly structure such as an oil tank or an old shed.

Climbers will also add height and take the eye to a focal point if they are given a pergola to clothe.

Patio overheads help to make the area seem more of an outdoor 'room', and climbers can help to achieve this effect, as well as providing shade.

CLIMBERS TO USE AS A SCREEN
Hedera helix (large-leaved varieties)*
Hedera colchica 'Dentata Variegata'*
Polygonum baldschuanicum
* evergreen

EVERGREEN WALL SHRUBS
Berberidopsis corallina (not suitable for chalky soils; needs sheltered position)
Ceanothus 'Delight' (one of the hardiest evergreen ceanothus)
Euonymus fortunei (syn. *E. radicans*)
Magnolia grandiflora (grows large; 'Exmouth' is a good form)

WALL SHRUBS FOR FRUIT
Berberidopsis corallina (not suitable for chalky soils; needs sheltered position)
Cotoneaster horizontalis
Pyracantha

WALL SHRUBS FOR FLOWER
Ceanothus 'Delight' (one of the hardiest evergreen ceanothus)
Chaenomeles speciosa and C. *superba* varieties

Ivy is a wonderful and vigorous climbing plant suitable for any wall. Hedera helix 'Jubilee' is illustrated.

CLIMBERS FOR PERGOLAS
Clematis montana and its varieties
Jasminum officinale
Lonicera periclymenum (and other climbing honeysuckles)
Roses, climbing
Vitis coignetiae (good autumn colour)

SELF-CLINGING CLIMBERS
Ampelopsis
Hedera helix varieties
Hydrangea petiolaris
Parthenocissus henryana
Parthenocissus quinquefolia
Parthenocissus tricuspidata
Pileostegia viburnoides
Trachelospermum jasminoides

CLIMBERS TO GROW FOR BOLD FLOWERS
Clematis, large-flowered hybrids
Clematis montana
Hydrangea petiolaris
Passiflora caerulea
Wisteria

CLIMBERS TO GROW INTO TREES
Rose 'Albertine', 'The Garland', 'Wedding Day', and R. *filipes* 'Kiftsgate'
Celastrus
Clematis
Hedera helix (choose an interesting variety such as the yellow-splashed 'Gold-heart' rather than a plain green one).
Hydrangea petiolaris

Ground Cover

Ground cover is not just something for people with large gardens; it is just as useful in a small garden to cover an area of ground that would otherwise need weeding, and in places where it is difficult to grow other plants – beneath trees for instance.

Ground cover is labour-saving, but only in the long term. Initially you will have to weed between the ground-cover plants while they are becoming established. That is why it is important to get the initial spacing right: if planted too far apart it may take many years before you achieve the desired effect – yet if planted too close it will be needlessly expensive, and you may soon have the work of thinning. The lists on this page give suitable spacings for some of the most useful ground cover plants.

Try not to regard ground cover as a merely functional type of planting. Many of the plants that can be used will enhance the garden in their own right, and using broad bands of a single plant often helps the garden design by offsetting the sometimes jumbled appearance that you can get with a lot of different plants in a small area.

Good ground preparation is essential if you want the plants to grow quickly in the early years and to achieve full cover as soon as possible. If you are using ground cover in difficult spots, such as beneath trees, it is especially important to make the ground hospitable. Wherever the ground is likely to become very dry, work in as much garden compost or peat as possible, and add some around the roots when you plant, and in all cases apply a general fertilizer at the rate recommended on the packet.

Ironically, it is also necessary to weed the ground first. Although the plants will eventually help to suppress weeds, they will not overcome *established* persistent perennial weeds. Annual weeds can be hoed off, but others are best treated with a suitable weedkiller (see page 135).

SOME SUITABLE PLANTS
In the lists of plants given on the left, the figures in brackets are the recommended planting distances. Plant in a triangular pattern so that the plants spread and knit together more effectively.

Be prepared to lift and divide herbaceous plants after about 10 years.

All the plants listed are evergreen except the ones marked with an asterisk (*).

FOR SHADE
Epimedium perralderanum (45 cm/1½ ft)
Galeobdolon luteum (syn. *Lamium galeobdolon*) 'Variegatum' (can be invasive) (60 cm/2 ft)
Hedera (*H. colchica* 'Dentata Variegata' looks brighter than most in shade) (90 cm/3 ft)
Hypericum calycinum (45 cm/1½ ft)
Pachysandra terminalis ('Variegata' is more attractive) (30 cm/1 ft)
Tiarella cordifolia (38 cm/15 in)

FOR DAMP AREAS (NOT WATERLOGGED)
Ajuga reptans (30 cm/1 ft)
Lysimachia nummularia (38 cm/15 in)

FOR DRY AREAS
Hebe pinguifolia 'Pagei' (38 cm/15 in)
Helianthemum nummularium varieties (38 cm/15 in)

FOR BANKS
Hedera colchica 'Dentata Variegata' (in sun or shade) (90 cm/3 ft)
Helianthemum nummularium varieties (in sun only) (38 cm/15 in)

CLUMP-FORMING PLANTS FOR GENERAL USE
These plants have a clump-forming habit, and are not likely to spread much.

Alchemilla mollis (38 cm/15 in)
Bergenia cordifolia (38 cm/15 in)
Saxifraga umbrosa (S. × *urbium*) (30 cm/1 ft)

Ajuga reptans, *rapidly spreading ground-cover.*

SPREADING PLANTS FOR GENERAL USE
Acaena microphylla (38 cm/15 in)
Ajuga reptans (30 cm/1 ft)
Cotoneaster dammeri (75 cm/2½ ft)
Euonymus fortunei varieties ('Emerald 'n' Gold' is a good one) (45 cm/1½ ft)
Geranium endressii 'Wargrave Pink' (38 cm/15 in)
Geranium macrorrhizum (38 cm/15 in)
Polygonum affine ('Donald Lowndes' and 'Darjeeling Red' are good varieties) (30 cm/1 ft)
Vinca minor (45 cm/1½ ft)
Waldsteinia ternata (30 cm/1 ft)

USING GROUND COVER

It is not necessary to keep to a single type of plant in one area. Try planting blocks of varieties with different colour foliage or flowers, or even completely different plants. If you go for a tapestry effect, you will have to match the plants' vigour as evenly as possible, otherwise one may gradually encroach upon the other's territory. This can be overcome to some extent by separating the blocks with a slower-growing but tough barrier plant such as bergenia.

Evergreen ground cover sounds attractive, but it can become dull and rather boring if it does not also have worthwhile flowers. Try underplanting with bulbs such as daffodils for spring flowering and colchicums for autumn interest. If using an ivy as cover for a sunny bank, try letting a large-flowered clematis sprawl through it to flower at ground level.

Besides the ground cover plants listed here, there are several prostrate conifers that can be used if you need something to look less like a ground cover planting yet still serve the same purpose. Those that you could try include *Juniperus communis* 'Repanda', J. *horizontalis*, J. *procumbens*, and J. *sabina* 'Tamariscifolia'

Heathers and Roses

Heathers make an effective as well as pretty ground cover once they have knitted together. They are also evergreen, and those with yellow or reddish foliage are pretty for most of the year. Roses can also be used as a ground cover, but of course they are decorative rather than weed-suppressing. If you want to try roses as ground cover, it is important to choose a suitable variety. Choose one such as 'Snow Carpet', 'The Fairy', or *Rosa × paulii*. Ground cover roses look best in a large garden where they have plenty of space.

Heathers make a most colourful ground cover which is effective throughout the year.

Using Rock Plants

It is not necessary to have a rock garden to grow rock plants. Some of the best alpines are grown in pots. Many of the more everyday plants are suitable for growing on or in walls, between paving, and even at the front of the herbaceous border. A gravel garden is an ideal setting for many of them. It is far better to place the plants where they will look right and do well, rather than be too concerned about using them in the rock garden simply because they are labelled as 'alpines'.

Whether you call them alpines or rock plants is more a case of horticultural snobbery than any essential practical difference. A true alpine is a plant that grows between the tree line and the permanent snow line, but a vast range of other plants are grown on rock gardens and the terms are used loosely to describe low-growing, compact plants suitable for growing on a rock garden (or in the case of the more delicate ones, in pots in a frame or alpine house, which is an unheated greenhouse with better than normal ventilation). But there are low shrubs such as sun roses (*Helianthemum nummularium*) that are equally at home on the rock garden, as ground cover for a sunny bank, or in a mixed border. And, of course, the truly dwarf conifers look particularly at home in a rock setting.

Plants in the rock garden A problem that often beats the experienced grower as well as the beginner is getting the balance right between vigorous plants and the more retiring types that are easily swamped. Some grow in tight, compact cushions, others rampage in all directions. If the rock garden is large enough you might be able to grow both extremes in different parts, otherwise it is best to decide on your priorities and choose the plants accordingly.

If you want good cover quickly, with a bright, bold show, go for the vigorous rock plants such as aubrieta, *Alyssum saxatile* and *Cerastium tomentosum*. Plants as vigorous as the latter will have to be cut back regularly, but this may be an acceptable price to pay for good covering power. What you should avoid are plants that are spreading yet difficult to control, such as *Sedum acre* – every tiny bit that breaks off seems to root and it will quickly become a weed that is difficult to eradicate. You can keep the colour going in this kind of rock garden with lots of dwarf bulbs, dwarf annuals and plants such as gazanias and mesembryanthemums. Dwarf conifers and dwarf shrubs can form the backbone planting.

If you are more interested in the miniature beauty of the individual plants, the cushion-forming and hummock-forming plants will probably appeal more, and you can amass a large collection in a relatively small area

Sedums and sempervivums are rock plants which look particularly attractive growing in crevices; usually non-invasive, there is a wide range to choose from.

Unfortunately some of the choice plants can become rather lost in a rock garden, so consider using them in raised beds, stone sinks, and other containers.

SOME ALPINES TO TRY

It is perfectly possible to grow plants from both the groups below on the same rock garden if it is large enough, but plants from the first group are likely to over-run single specimens or more dainty types, so take care when using them. The second group should hold its own with the first yet not swamp individuals.

BOLD AND VIGOROUS ROCK PLANTS

Ajuga reptans and varieties
Alyssum saxatile
Aster alpinus
Aubrieta deltoidea varieties
Campanula garganica
Cerastium tomentosum
Geranium subcaulescens
Phlox douglasii
Phlox subulata
Polygonum vacciniifolium
Saponaria ocymoides

SPREADING OR LAX HABIT, BUT USEFUL AND EASILY CONTROLLED

Acaena microphylla
Aethionema 'Warley Rose'
Androsace sarmentosa
Antennaria alpina
Antennaria dioica
Arabis ferdinandi-coburgi 'Variegata'
Arenaria balearica
Campanula cochleariifolia
Dianthus deltoides and varieties
Diascia cordata
Dryas octopetala
Erinus alpinus
Gypsophila repens
Potentilla tabernaemontani
Silene schafta
Veronica prostrata

A well established rock garden on a sloping site, which makes it easier to appreciate the plants. The plants include Veronica gentianoides, Phlox subulata, *and* Cotyledon simplicifolia.

DWARF SHRUBS TO TRY

Acer palmatum varieties (will grow large eventually, but is slow-growing)
Berberis buxifolia 'Nana'
Berberis thunbergii 'Atropurpurea Nana'
Calluna vulgaris varieties (choose the dwarfest)
Ceratostigma plumbaginoides
Cotoneaster dammeri
Cytisus × *beanii*
Cytisus × *kewensis*
Daphne cneorum
Erica herbacea (syn. *E. carnea*)
Genista lydia
Hebe pinguifolia 'Pagei'
Helianthemum nummularium varieties
Hypericum olympicum
Iberis sempervirens 'Little Gem'
Lithospermum diffusum 'Heavenly Blue'
Rhododendron (dwarf varieties such as 'Blue Tit')

ROCK GARDEN CONIFERS

Many conifers sold as 'dwarf' will grow too large for most rock gardens. There are many more suitable conifers than the ones below, but make sure they really are true dwarfs or pygmy varieties before you plant them.

DWARF CONIFERS

Abies balsamea 'Hudsonia'
Chamaecyparis lawsoniana 'Minima Aurea' and 'Minima Glauca'
Chamaecyparis obtusa 'Nana Aurea' and 'Nana Gracilis'
Juniperus communis 'Compressa'
Juniperus communis 'Depressa Aurea'
Picae abies 'Nidiformis'
Picea glauca 'Albertiana Conica'
Thuja orientalis 'Rosedalis'
Thuja orientalis 'Aurea Nana'

Plants for the Water Garden

Most gardens benefit from a water feature, though in a formal garden a pool that depends on shape and perhaps a fountain or cascade may have no plants and still be successful. Usually, however, ponds are installed as much for the pleasure of enjoying fish and water plants as for their contribution to garden design.

It is hard to imagine a collection of aquatic plants without waterlilies, but it is often the marginal plants around the edge of the pond that give it a well-planted look for most of the season.

There are hundreds of good plants to choose from, but as with the rock garden, there are some that it is best to avoid as they are likely to be difficult to control.

Plants to avoid range from the tiny duckweeds (Lemna spp) to the great reed mace (Typha latifolia). They include the yellow pond lily (Nuphar lutea), yellow flag (Iris pseudacorus), bur reed (Sparganium ramosum), and the reed mace (Typha angustifolia).

Waterlilies are a 'must'. They tend to be expensive, but normally last for many years without difficulty. Choose those suitable for the depth of water above the crown.

There are other deep-water plants for the centre of the pool or where the water is at full depth, although often it need not be deeper than about 30 cm/1 ft, but high on the list after a waterlily must be the water hawthorn (Aponogeton distachyus). It has curious, white, forked flowers with black anthers, blooming freely in early summer and sporadically through into autumn. Its floating strap-shaped leaves are almost evergreen. It is also fragrant, but you will probably have to risk falling into the pond to appreciate the scent.

Next choose your 'marginal' plants – those for the shallow water areas at the edge of the pool. This is much more difficult than choosing plants for the centre of the pool: there are many more species from which to choose, and their requirements and growth habits vary.

The submerged oxygenating plants are among the most important for the biological balance of the pool. They do not contribute much to the visual impact of the garden, so it is best to choose those that do the job efficiently without becoming a nuisance. Start with those that are also visually interesting such as Callitriche palustris (syn. C. verna) Ceratophyllum demersum (hornwort), Hottonia palustris (water violet), Myriophyllum spicatum and M. verticillatum (both milfoils), and Tillaea recurva. Also useful as oxygenators, but less attractive, are Ranunculus aquatilis (water crowfoot) and

Plenty of marginal plants will help to soften the edge of the pool and make it look more natural.

Lagarosiphon major (syn. *Elodea crispa*). Avoid the more rampant elodeas such as *Elodea canadensis* (Canadian pond-weed).

A SHORTLIST OF WATERLILIES
The figures in brackets are the preferred depth of water above the crown.

FOR A MINIATURE POND
'Pymaea Alba' (white, 10–23 cm/4–9 in)
'Pygmaea Helvola' (yellow, 10–23 cm/4–9 in)

FOR A SMALL POND
'Froebeli' (red, 15–45 cm/6–18 in)
'Laydekeri Lilacea' (pink, 10–30 cm/4–12 in)
'Laydekeri Purpurata' (red, 15–45 cm/6–18 in)
'Rose Arey' (pink, 23–45 cm/9–18 in)

FOR A MEDIUM OR LARGE POND
'Albatross' (white, 15–45 cm/6–18 in)
'James Brydon' (red, 30–60 cm (12–24 in)
'Marliacea Chromatella' (yellow, 30–75 cm/12–30 in)
'Mme Wilfron Gonnêre' (pink, 23–45 cm/9–18 in)
'Odorata Alba' (white, 23–45 cm/9–18 in)
'Rene Gerard' (red, 23–60 cm/9–24 in)

PLANTS FOR THE MARGINS
The following list is a selection of the most decorative and easy to grow. Try selecting from these first, then if you have space for more, try some of the other marginal plants.

Acorus calamus 'Variegatus'
Caltha palustris 'Flore Pleno' ('Plena')
Iris laevigata (good varieties are 'Atropurpurea', 'Colchesteri', 'Mottled Beauty', 'Snowdrift', and 'Variegata')
Iris versicolor
Orontium aquaticum
Pontederia cordata
Sagittaria japonica 'Plena' ('Flore Pleno')
Scirpus tabernaemontani 'Zebrinus' (syn. S. zebrinus)

Plants Around the Pond
Plants described as bog plants are suitable for growing in the wet, marshy, ground around the edge of a natural pool. Most garden ponds have a watertight edge, however, and the ground an inch from the edge will be as dry as the rest of the garden, so bear this in mind when planting.

Fortunately many border plants will associate well visually with water, and will often grow better if the ground is damp. The following are all worth trying, but those marked with an asterisk (*) will require either a proper bog garden, or ground with plenty of peat and garden compost added as well as being regularly flooded.

Astilbe hybrids
Gunnera manicata (a focal-point plant, but it requires plenty of space and winter protection for the crown)
Hemerocallis hybrids
Iris kaempferi and its varieties
Iris pallida 'Variegata'
Lobelia cardinalis (or L. fulgens)
Lobelia vedrariensis
Lysichitum americanum
Lysichitum camtschatcense
Mimulus hybrids
Peltiphyllum peltatum
Primula florindae
Rheum palmatum 'Rubrum'
Schizostylis coccinea
Trollius hybrids

Below *Check levels regularly when making a garden pool. It's especially vital to get the edge of the pool level all round, otherwise there will be a lip of the liner showing once the water has found the true level, and it will be difficult to disguise.*
Bottom left *Spread a layer of sand over the base, sides and ledges, to even out irregularities and to reduce the chance of sharp stones damaging the liner.*
Bottom right *Spread the liner loosely over the hole, weighting the edges, and let the water take it into the contours. Some folds will be visible at first, but you probably won't notice them once the pond has been planted.*

Using Containers

Growing plants in containers is labour-intensive as they will need watering and tending more often than plants in the ground. It is also expensive – the plants usually have to be replaced frequently and the containers themselves are costly. But windowboxes, tubs, and troughs can bring colour and interest to parts of the garden that would otherwise probably be uninteresting. Containers can be decorative in their own right and they will also solve the problem of growing plants in difficult situations.

A surprising range of plants can be grown successfully in this restricted way, including plants as unlikely as mimulus and hostas, both of which are usually regarded as intolerant of dry roots, and there are lots of dwarf shrubs and conifers that can be used. Summer bedding and spring bulbs have their place, but do not overlook the perennials, many of which have a long season of interest and will not need to be replaced once or twice a year.

If the container is to form a focal point, plan for permanency, using a small tree or large shrub, which should remain small for some years with such a restrained root system. You could also grow fruit such as figs, peaches, or apples in tubs (make sure an apple has a dwarfing rootstock).

Some conifers make good tub plants if you choose suitable species and varieties. Single conifers can look rather rigid, however, so try mixing several with different outlines in one large container. Try a rounded *Chamaecyparis obtusa*, a prostrate *Juniperus horizontalis* and an upright *Juniperus communis* 'Hibernica' together for instance.

Architectural plants such as *Agave americana*, a *Chamaerops humilis*, or a *Trachycarpus fortunei* will make a feature in a *large* container (but these will all need protection in cold areas). Hardy, but equally impressive in a large tub, is the false castor oil plant, *Fatsia japonica*.

Other useful evergreen shrubs that can make handsome plants in tubs include camellias and dwarf rhododendrons (try the R. *yakushimanum* hybrids), and of course a clipped bay.

Herbaceous border plants are less versatile as container plants because they have summer-only interest, unless you use something like bergenias, which are evergreen. For summer interest, try agapanthus (may need winter protection), hostas, and *Nepeta* × *faassenii*.

Left The smaller the space, the more effective plants can be. This city garden has been created in a narrow raised bed on the pavement.
Right Petunias in a container.

Lawns

For many gardeners, a neat, striped lawn is the ideal centrepiece to complement the rest of the garden. If you have lots of time, are prepared to spend money and effort on it, and do not have children that will want to treat it as a recreation area, the lawn can be one of the main focal points of the garden, and the envy of your neighbours.

Be Realistic

As few of us can manage this combination of attributes, however, it may be better to settle for a more realistic objective.

A lawn does not have to look like a bowling green, or even be weed-free, to be effective. If you have a large garden with informal shrub borders, for instance, fairly coarse grasses and even a fair sprinkling of daisies and other weeds may be perfectly acceptable. If the lawn is very large, there is a lot to be said for leaving some areas of grass deliberately long to allow wild flowers to grow and to encourage wildlife. Provided the areas are well defined and appear intentional, they will look interesting rather than neglected.

For most people the lawn is a more modest affair, and it probably has to serve as a play and sitting-out area as well as a setting for beds and borders. For these, a lush green, hard-wearing surface is more important than a close-cut banded finish. One of the so-called hard-wearing grass seed mixtures containing rye grass should be perfectly adequate, and need not be synonymous with coarseness. Earlier strains of rye grass could be rather coarse but modern varieties are far superior and produce a relatively fine, close-knit lawn. And with modern rotary and hover

Although a lawn inevitably means quite a lot of work during the summer months, it makes the perfect complement to other garden features.

mowers, the long flowering stalks are no longer a problem to cut.

And if you do not want weeds, it is not difficult to get rid of them (see page 135).

If you are planning to make a new lawn, consider both ease of mowing and the effect of wear as well as the overall integration with the other garden features. Avoid too many awkward corners or complicated beds that will make mowing tricky and create more edges to be trimmed. Keep the sweeps gradual, and avoid narrow areas that are going to take a lot of wear. A few large beds will probably be more effective than a lot of little ones.

Do not try to shape the edges as you sow or lay the turf. The results will be more successful, and the job easier, if you sow or lay the turfs in a straight line, overlapping the area you want to curve. Once the grass is established, it is easy to cut the edges back to any desired contour.

Size and Shape

In a large garden, lawns are really the only practical way to fill a large area of ground. In a very small garden it is worth considering some alternatives. In the majority of gardens, however, it is desirable to make a feature of the lawn without allowing it to dominate the design. Like hedges, the lawn should form an attractive background to the main ornamental plants in the garden.

Making a Lawn

Whether you are sowing seed or laying turf, it is worth spending time and effort on preparing the ground well. Ground preparation is less important for turf, but even if it is only for a play lawn you still want a reasonably level and smooth surface to mow.

Preparing the Ground

Always dig the ground thoroughly first – it is the only chance you will get. It makes sense to remove as many perennial weeds as possible, but you can always resort to weedkillers later. Pay special attention to coarse grasses as these cannot be tackled with a selective weedkiller once the lawn is established.

Prepare the ground in plenty of time – a month or two before you sow or turf if possible. This will allow weed seeds to germinate and be killed, and the ground will have settled so that depressions can be filled and levelled.

It should be possible to hoe off any annual weeds that emerge, but you could use a non-residual contact weedkiller; if there are difficult perennial weeds too, use a systemic weedkiller such as glyphosate (allow a couple of weeks to elapse before sowing). Modern selective weedkillers will control most weeds after the lawn is established, but there is no point in starting off at a disadvantage.

If the area is very poorly drained, and water tends to lie on the surface after heavy rain, you may need to improve

Alternatives to Grass?

The drawback to grass is not its appearance, but its maintenance. Plant alternatives to grass are not without problems, however, for though they might be good to *look* at, they are unlikely to tolerate wear in the way that most grasses can.

Chamomile is the alternative most commonly suggested. Unfortunately it is difficult to establish, and far from the labour-saving proposition that you might think. You can use a selective weedkiller on a grass lawn, so that the weeds are killed while the grass is left unharmed. There is no such happy solution to the weed problem in a chamomile lawn (though you can kill couch grass with alloxydim sodium without harming the chamomile.

Choose a non-flowering chamomile, otherwise it will need trimming occasionally with the mower set high to prevent it flowering.

Thyme is the other main contender, but choose a creeping form (*Thymus serpyllum*). It will need occasional trimming to keep it neat and, as with chamomile, weeds can be a problem.

Although thyme is no substitute for a main lawn, it may be worth trying it for a very small ornamental area where the drawbacks are worth coping with for the decorative and fragrant benefits.

Gravel is not so nice to walk, or lie, on, but as a low-maintenance alternative for a small lawn it has considerable merits. Weeds are easily controlled with a once-a-year application of a path weedkiller, and you can plant through the gravel if you want to add interest. Gravel makes a very 'sympathetic' background for plants.

Paving and decking Although not suitable for a large area, wooden decking or stone paving will make a really easy-to-maintain garden if you avoid too many containers. Both can be expensive initially, however.

A wide variety of material is available: stone slabs or flags, tiles, bricks, concrete and wood.

This picture shows how effective a garden can be without grass. And apart from a few containers to water regularly it has the bonus of needing the minimum of maintenance. This oasis of a garden gives the impression of tranquillity, and is packed with character, despite its small size. You need to think creatively to design a garden like this, but if you want a garden of character, it may pay to dismiss the traditional lawn and borders as a starting point.

the drainage. Laying proper land drains is very heavy and tedious work, and in many small gardens it is difficult to find a suitable area into which to let them drain (do not simply run the water into your neighbour's garden). Modern drainage systems are available that require only a narrow and relatively shallow excavation, and it may be worth considering these. If you have a minor drainage problem, laying the lawn on a gentle slope may be enough (1:50 is adequate and should hardly be noticeable). If the ground is really badly drained, consider whether that part of the garden could better be used for some other purpose, such as making a natural bog garden, or for growing a collection of moisture-loving plants.

If the ground has been allowed to settle, and raked level a few times, it should not be necessary to roll it.

If you are going to need to lay electricity cables or water pipes across the lawn, be sure to do so before you sow or lay the turf.

Step-by-step sowing Late summer or early autumn is the best time to sow a lawn, as the ground will be warm but should not be too dry during the early stages of growth. Seed can be sown successfully in spring, but unless the season is very wet you will probably have to water it regularly until the grass is established.

● Level the ground carefully. You may be able to do this by eye, but if the area is small and you want to be sure of the level, use a spirit-level on a straight-edge between pegs. When all the pegs are at the same height, rake the ground level between them (if the ground is uneven, make a mark about 2.5–5 cm (1–2 in) from the top of each peg and level the ground to these marks).

● Tread the ground to consolidate it, shuffling over the area with the feet close together (it's best to do this when the ground is fairly dry).

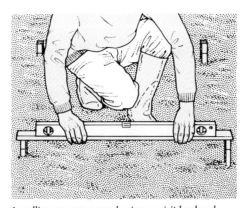

Levelling uneven ground using a spirit level and straight edge. Mark the pegs an inch from the top.

● A week before sowing, sprinkle on an autumn lawn fertilizer, and if the ground is very sandy work plenty of damp peat into the top 8 cm (3 in) of soil.

● After about a week, hoe off any seedlings that have appeared, rake level again, and mark the ground into yard or metre strips, using string or canes.

● Sow half the recommended rate first then apply the other half in strips at right angles to the first. This should ensure an even distribution of the seed.

Sowing rates for the various mixtures are indicated on the packaging. Scatter the seed with a swirling motion, high enough from the ground so that it does not fall too thickly.

● Rake the seed in *lightly* – it should not be covered by more than 6 mm (¼ in) of soil otherwise germination is likely to be inhibited.

Black cotton stretched over the area may help to deter birds from having dust baths, but to reduce seed losses try treated seed (it should be unpalatable, but it may not make a lot of difference). If you use a bird scarer, move it about or use several types in turn so that the birds don't become too familiar with them.

● Water the ground thoroughly if it is dry, and keep irrigated until the grass is established.

Seed or turf?

Whether it is best to start with seed or turf depends on what you want from your lawn, how much you are prepared to spend, how much effort you are prepared to put in, and how much patience you have.

CHOOSE TURF IF YOU:

● want quick results

● do not mind the expense

● do not mind which grasses it contains (you can buy turf specially cultivated from fine grasses, but it is much more expensive)

● are able to inspect the turf first, or are prepared to spend money on weed-killers if necessary (quality may be less important if you simply want a play lawn)

CHOOSE SEED IF YOU:

● want to save money (turf may be ten times more expensive for a given area.)

● do not mind waiting for results (it may be three to six months before you can use it)

● want to choose a grass mixture for a specific purpose

Laying turf Follow the ground preparation advice for sowing seed, but you do not have to be so thorough. If the turf has arrived, do not delay – lay it as soon as possible.

Mid and late autumn are the best times to lay turf, but you can get away with it at any time during the winter provided the ground is not frozen or waterlogged. It can be laid successfully in spring but you will need to water it more often. Summer is not a good time because the turf is more likely to dry out.

• Lay the first row of turf against a straight line, then place a wooden plank on the grass already laid and stand on this while you work on the next row.

• Stagger the joints so that those in one row do not coincide with those in the previous one. The turves should look rather like bonded brickwork.

• Butt each turf as closely as possible to the previous one, and firm it down well with the back of a spade.

• When the turf has been laid, brush in a topdressing mixture (four parts sand, two parts soil, one part peat) between the joints.

• Trim the edges as necessary, then water thoroughly and do not let the grass dry out until it has become established.

About Grasses
You can get a good idea of the types of grass contained in a seed mixture from the seedman's description, or its name. The mixtures intended for a fine lawn are likely to contain Chewing's red fescue, probably creeping red fescue, and maybe bent. A few might also contain rough-stalked meadow grass or smooth-stalked meadow grass.

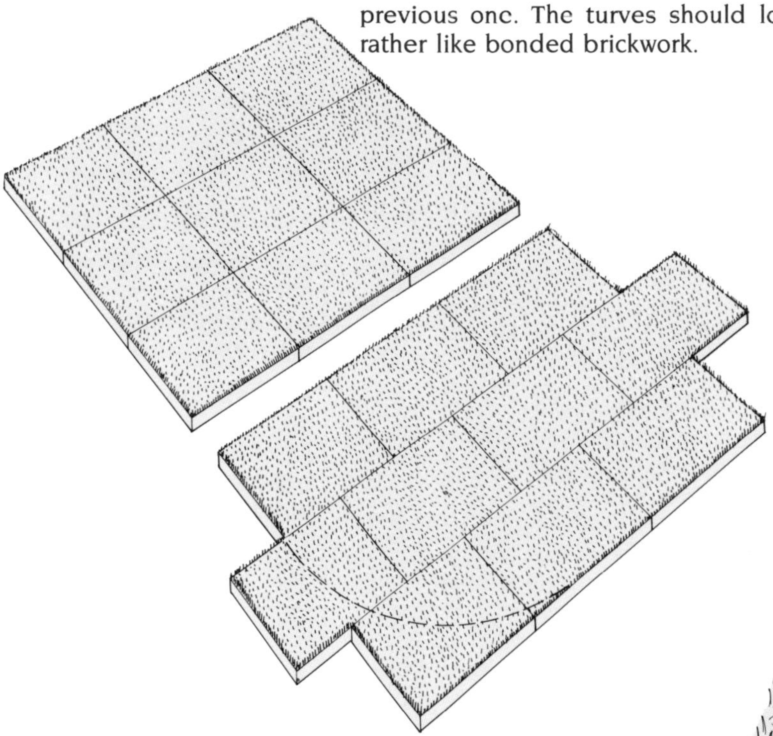

When laying turves, stagger the joins as shown below left (top left is incorrect). This helps them to knit together more strongly. Cut the edge to the desired shape after the lawn has been laid and brush on a dressing of sand, soil and peat, or work it in with the back of a rake.

Mixtures intended for shade are likely to vary widely from one seedsman to another, and may contain species such as *Poa nemoralis* (wood meadow grass), or hard fescue. You may find that an ordinary grass mixture does just as well – provided you avoid too much wear (try stepping stones set into the lawn in areas walked across most often).

You may also be able to buy mixtures for damp areas or dry areas, but these may not be much better than ordinary mixtures. A grass that does well in one lawn may do poorly in another. Often, with any lawn, some of the grasses in a mixture will die out, while different grasses may fail to establish on a lawn in another area. Also, other grasses may eventually seed themselves.

Hard-wearing lawn mixtures usually contain rye grass. Some contain only rye grass, but most are mixed with other grasses such as creeping red fescue. The variety of rye grass used is likely to vary from one seedsman or mixture to another, some such as 'Hunter' and 'Sprinter' – are dwarf, relatively fine grasses that are far superior to some of the older varieties of perennial rye grass. Others to look out for include 'Arno', 'Manhattan', and 'Score'.

A mixture of fine fescues and bents will produce the best quality lawn as they have fine leaves, are low-growing, and tolerate close mowing. Because they are slow-growing they tend to need mowing less often than more vigorous grasses, but it means that you have to be more patient while the lawn is becoming established.

If you want a lawn that will establish quickly, take hard wear, and compete more effectively with weeds, choose one containing a good perennial rye grass. If you use a cylinder mower, however, you will probably find that the flowering stalks of rye grass tend to get missed by the blades – though this is not a problem if you use a wheeled rotary or a hover mower.

The Neglected Lawn

If you have an existing lawn that is looking the worse for wear, or simply lacks the appearance of a good, healthy lawn, there is a lot that can be done to improve it. Even if the shape is wrong, it may be possible to lift sections and replace them elsewhere. This is preferable to sowing new seed to extend it or to fill in old flower beds.

Usually, however, the problem is not with the shape of the lawn, but its condition. These are some of the problems, and solutions to them:

Uneven Surface
Within limits you can level off an uneven lawn by filling in the depressions and lowering the bumps.

Bumps are best dealt with by making an H-shaped cut over the bump, using a half-moon edger (you can use a spade, but the cuts will not be as straight). Roll back the flaps produced by undercutting from the cross-bar of the H, remove some soil, then replace the flaps.

Hollows can be filled gradually by adding about 12 mm (½ in) of sifted soil and peat over the grass and repeating it again later if necessary.

Broken Edges
The simplest solution is to trim back the edge with a half-moon edger (a spade is likely to produce a slightly scalloped finish). Unfortunately if you continue with this approach over a number of years the beds get bigger and the lawn smaller. Try removing a rectangle of turf and reversing it so that the damaged edge is on the inside. You can then brush fine soil into any gaps and reseed if necessary.

Coarse Grasses Predominate
It is impossible to make a quality lawn out of coarse grasses, so you will have to live with the constraints unless you are prepared to dig the lawn up and start again.

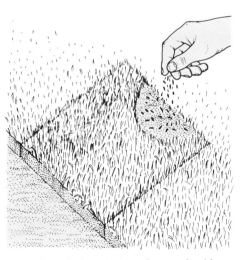

Reseeding a broken edge after the piece of turf has been reversed.

The overall quality can be improved by feeding in spring and summer, and keeping the grass cut to about 2.5 cm (1 in); close mowing favours the growth of the finer grasses, but if you have a predominance of coarse grasses the whole lawn may suffer if you cut closer than this. If the lawn is of predominantly fine grass with patches of coarse grass, try mowing to 18 mm (¾ in); this should favour the fine species and deter the stronger ones.

Weed Problems

If the lawn is large and informal, it is probably best to learn to live with some weeds. They can look perfectly acceptable in some settings. It is on a small, high quality lawn that even a few dandelions will be conspicuous.

Almost all lawn weeds can be controlled relatively easily by using selective (hormone) lawn weedkillers (see page 135). Do not expect to kill all the weeds with one application – a second attempt is usually necessary. If a few difficult weeds remain after the second treatment, a spot weeder (aerosol or wipe-on stick) should finish them off.

Do not despise hand weeding. If there are just a few weeds, hand weeding can be quick, simple and cheaper than the alternatives.

Moss

Moss thrives when conditions are poor. Mosskillers will help to achieve short-term control, but moss will probably return unless you improve the overall conditions.

Get rid of the moss to start with: rake out as much as possible (a powered lawn rake should be very effective and will save a lot of effort if the lawn is large). Use a mosskiller such as lawn sand (this is a mixture of iron and a nitrogenous fertilizer in a sand carrier – you can make your own but it is easier to buy it ready-mixed) in early autumn, followed by a second dose in spring. There are also mosskillers that you can water on, and they often contain a fertilizer to give the grass a boost, but none of these is likely to have a lasting effect.

Mosskillers containing chloroxuron prevent moss for a longer period, but are likely to be more expensive.

Once the immediate problem is under control try to prevent the moss returning by:

● feeding the grass

● aerating the lawn (spiking it, and brushing in sand if the drainage is poor)

● not mowing too closely

● avoiding shade if possible (you may be able to cut back overhanging trees or shrubs casting a lot of shade)

The appearance of this lawn would be improved if the brown areas are aerated by spiking and then fed with a lawn fertilizer.

Mowing Tips

- Always make sure the blades are set to the correct height for the type of grass and time of year. Check the instruction manual if you are unsure of the method to use.

- Keep the blades sharp.

- Try to avoid cutting wet grass.

- If the mower is sharp, and you have not let the grass grow too long, mow with smooth movements – it should not be necessary to keep going over the same piece of grass using the mower as you might a carpet sweeper.

- If you want a 'lined' finish, mow across the ends first, then mow along the lawn in alternating directions (use a mower with a roller to get a good striped effect).

- Occasionally cut the grass in the opposite direction (across the lawn instead of along it). It should not be necessary to mow diagonally.

Leaving areas of grass long can reduce the amount of mowing.

Keeping it Cut

Although cutting the grass is less of a chore than it used to be before the days of relatively inexpensive powered mowers, it is still time-consuming. Making the job as easy as possible will give more time to enjoy the rest of the garden.

How Short, How Often?

Few of us can expect to achieve a lawn with a bowling-green finish. It is impossible unless you start with the right grasses, mow perhaps three or four times a week in summer, and feed regularly. Even then you will need the right kind of mower.

Most gardeners are content with a tidy, neatly cut lawn, free from very coarse grasses, with a good green colour. If you have children you will probably want one that is hard wearing into the bargain.

Purely ornamental lawns containing fine grasses should not need cutting more often than once a week in summer to remain respectable – but do not cut it too short in the belief that it will need cutting less frequently. Close but infrequent mowing usually leaves the grass looking uneven before cutting and pale afterwards. Few ordinary ornamental lawns need cutting closer than 18 mm (¾ in) in summer. Leave the grass longer in spring and autumn.

Although a rectangular lawn is easier to mow, it will look more interesting with one or two island beds – they needn't be round or planted with annuals, kidney-shaped or oval beds planted with perennials are very effective. Curved borders are also generally more effective than too many straight lines.

If you have a hard-wearing lawn containing rye grass, which does not generally respond well to very close cutting, aim for a summer cutting height of 25 mm (1 in). Mowing every seven to ten days should be adequate during most of the growing season.

Collecting the Clippings

Some gardeners prefer to collect the clippings because they believe that letting them lie on the ground causes a harmful 'thatch'. This is unlikely to be a problem except on a very high quality lawn where you do not want worm casts (and in any case the thatch will be removed if you use a lawn rake); for most lawns leaving the clippings on will not normally do any harm if the lawn is cut regularly.

It is worth collecting the clippings from the first cut in spring (when the grass is usually long) and if the weather is wet (the clippings may lie like a blanket instead of shrivelling, and cause the grass beneath to turn yellow). You may also want to collect them if you are concerned about the clippings treading into the house. But do not feel

Mower Safety

Mowers – especially powered mowers – are potentially dangerous, and many people are injured by them each year. Some are killed.

It is well worth introducing a residual current device into the circuit. Those that you use at an individual socket are relatively inexpensive for the protection that they give; one that protects a whole circuit will be useful for other equipment too.

To reduce the risk of injury from the mower being turned on accidentally while you are cleaning or attending to it (a common cause of accidents), choose one with a lock-off (not lock-on) switch.

Many injuries are also caused by the blade on rotary mowers cutting limbs, and hazardous accidents happen when the cable gets cut. Some of the newer models have plastic blades, which are likely to cause less damage to you, and that will take longer to cut through a cable. It is well worth considering these. Replacement blades are inexpensive.

Whatever type of mower you use, cutting grass on slopes is hazardous. You could try cutting across the slope so that there is less chance of the mower falling on to you if you fall, but better still avoid having grass on steep slopes.

that you have to use a grass collector: if you don't you will save on the time and effort of emptying it, and the nutrients will be recycled so you will probably not have to feed the grass so often.

Some gardeners worry about weed or grass seeds being spread if the clippings are not collected, but trials have shown that this is unlikely to be a problem – especially if the grass is cut regularly.

Which Mower?

Competing claims from manufacturers and the blurring of distinctions between types (some rotary mowers now have rear rollers, and there are hover mowers with grass collectors, for instance) can make choosing the right mower a difficult decision.

If you have more than about 250 sq m (300 sq yd) of lawn to cut:

● Consider a petrol cylinder mower or a rotary mower with a rear roller if you want a striped lawn.

● Consider a petrol wheeled rotary or hover mower if the stripes are not important. If the lawn is very large, a rotary mower with powered wheels will be useful, but these are more expensive.

If you have less than about 250 sq m (300 sq yd) of lawn to cut:

● Consider a hand mower if the lawn is small and you want the exercise. If you want stripes, choose a rear–roller mower. If stripes are unimportant consider a side-wheeled mower (likely to be lighter to push, but it will be more difficult to mow up to the edge of a flower bed).

● If you do not want a hand mower, consider an electric cylinder mower or a rotary mower with a rear roller if you want stripes. Consider an electric wheeled rotary or hover mower if you are not bothered about stripes.

Other jobs

Raking/scarifying is one of the most useful jobs after mowing. It will help to raise the creeping or horizontal growth that is usually missed by cylinder mowers, it will help to reduce moss, and should discourage trailing weeds such as clover. It will also prevent a 'thatch' building up on the surface, which can restrict root growth and encourage moss. If the lawn is large, consider buying a powered lawn rake.

Aeration is necessary on an average type of lawn only if the ground is poorly drained or if the surface is very compacted (from playing sports for instance). On a typical lawn it should not be necessary more than once every two or three years. A proper aerator that takes out a core of soil is ideal, but slitters (some of which can be attached to some mowers) may be more convenient. Spiking the lawn with a fork can be satisfactory, but it is hard and tedious work.

Topdressing helps to create a level surface and fill in small dents, but on most lawns these probably do not matter. Autumn, perhaps after aerating, is a good time to apply a topdressing. Brush in a mixture of equal parts pit or river sand and sieved soil if the ground is heavy, equal parts peat and sieved soil if the ground is light and sandy.

A spring-tined lawn rake – useful for a small area.

Lawn Problems

Diseases Some of the most serious lawn problems are caused by fungi that attack the grass:

Fusarium patch is one of the most common lawn diseases in Britain. The first signs are usually small, dark brown patches, which gradually enlarge and merge. Pink cottonwool-like growth can sometimes be seen.

Use a systemic fungicide such as benomyl or thiophanate-methyl when the grass is growing actively, improve drainage if necessary, avoid too much shade, and do not use too much nitrogenous fertilizer.

Red thread is another common disease, usually noticed in summer or autumn. There are patches of pale brown grass, and closer inspection should reveal coral-red strands of fungus.

Control is usually possible with fungicides such as benomyl or thiphanate-methyl. Feeding the lawn should help the grass to recover and reduce the chance of a further attack.

Fairy rings look interesting, but they are a serious problem. The fungus creates an area of lush growth (usually in a ring formation), sometimes with poor or dying grass inside. Sometimes small toadstools appear, usually in late summer or autumn. With the mildest form, the grass will look uneven, with a bad infestation it may be killed.

You can try sulphate of iron (400 g to 4.5 litres of water over 2 sq m/12 oz to a gallon of water over 2 sq yd). The only certain way to eliminate it is to remove the turf, extending about 30 cm (1 ft) beyond the ring, and water the soil with a 2 per cent formalin solution (you should be able to buy this from a chemist). Wait for a month before reseeding or laying turf.

Pests There are relatively few pests to worry about:

Worms are only a problem if the casts become flattened and act as a seedbed

Fairy rings, a descriptive common name for the disease caused by various fungi. The visible symptoms depend on the stage of development, but there is usually an area of lush grass around the edge of the circle of poor growth.

for weed seeds; they also affect aeration. If you want to use a fairly safe method of control, use derris dust or potassium permanganate (32 g to 4.5 litres of water per sq m/1 oz to 4 pints of water per sq yd), though these have the drawback of bringing the worms to the surface and may not always kill them, so you have to gather them up. Worm-killers based on carbaryl are more effective but have to be used with more care.

Leatherjackets are a more serious problem. Irregular yellowish patches, often first noticed in dry weather, are a sign of leatherjackets eating the roots. Use soil insecticides such as bromophos or diazinon, but gamma-HCH dust applied in mid autumn, or in mild weather in spring, is usually successful.

APPENDIX
Plant Health

This is the chapter that everyone hopes there will be no need to refer to. But ignoring problems will not make them go away, and recognizing trouble at an early stage, and taking the right action promptly, can turn a potential disaster into a minor inconvenience.

Considering Plant Health

You can turn plant health into a challenging aspect of your hobby – being your own plant doctor and prescribing the right treatment can become an interest rather than a chore. That is *not* a recommendation that you should be over-generous with the use of pesticides; as with human ailments, prevention is often better than cure, and good garden hygiene and healthy growing conditions can reduce the need for pesticides. Sometimes, as with cabbage root fly, there are simple precautions that provide effective control without chemicals.

Pest and disease control should be taken seriously. It is no fun growing apples for the benefit of the codling moth maggots or carrots for the grubs of the carrot root fly. It is a waste of time, effort, and money, if the crops have to be thrown away because they are inedible. And in the flower garden the effects can be just as devastating: nobody wants earwig-eaten dahlias, eelworm-ridden phlox, or virus-stunted chrysanthemums.

A Plan of Campaign
There are so many possible pests that you *could* encounter that the list would be depressingly long, and give the false impression that growing plants is a difficult business. In fact, you are unlikely even to encounter some of the relatively common pests and diseases that you will read about in books and magazines, so it is important to keep things in perspective. Included here are the main types of insect and disease that you might have to cope with. They are described under categories relating to the parts of a plant and dealing with the sort of damage caused. Even if you encounter some of the less common insects or diseases, you should be able to decide on the appropriate treatment by analogy.

It is also important to recognize some of the beneficial insects that you might find in the garden, so that you do not destroy these. Some of the more common ones are given on page 131.

Decide which of the following categories fits the pest most closely, and even if you cannot be precise about the diagnosis you will probably be able to take the right steps to rectify it.

Houseplants are beyond the scope of this book, and although it should still be possible to use the information to diagnose some of the problems, others due to the home environment (such as scorched leaves due to too much direct sunlight through the glass, or brown leaf tips due to lack of humidity) are too uncommon on outdoor plants to be included here. You also need to be careful about using some of our suggested insecticides indoors. Some of them have an unpleasant smell, others may mark furnishings, a few might be too dangerous to use safely in the home. It's best to buy products intended for use in the home.

Useful Viruses

Despite the recommendation to destroy virus-infected plants, not all viruses do the plant any real harm and they can contribute to a plant's decorative value. Some variegated plants in which the colour breaking and streaking are caused by viruses – 'broken' tulips (those with flecked petals), and the variegated abutilon used as a bedding plant are examples – are propagated and cultivated. As a general rule, however, do not save or propagate virus-infected plants unless it is usual to do so.

Leaf Problems

It is usually leaves that show the first signs of stress, but sometimes the trouble lies not with the leaf itself but with other parts of the plant such as the roots. Leaves can assume an unusual colouring because of nutritional deficiencies, or the action of insects feeding on the roots, and they may wilt because the root system is damaged and the plant cannot take up enough water. Usually, however, the leaves are eaten or malformed in some way.

If you can see insects or other pests on the leaves . . .
Decide whether they are chewing insects or sap-suckers.

● If the leaves have holes in them, caterpillars of some kind are the most likely cause, and the culprit will almost always be easily visible if you look carefully. Beetles of various kinds are another possibility, especially weevils, though you may not actually find the beetle on the plants unless you look at the right time.

Slugs and snails are other common culprits. If the actual pest is not visible look for the slime trails left behind.

Control: For caterpillars, try permethrin with heptenophos (systemic), carbaryl, HCH, or derris. For beetles such as weevils, try fenitrothion, HCH, resmethrin, or pyrethrum. For slugs and snails try baits based on metaldehyde or methiocarb.

● If the leaves do not have holes in them, the chances are the insects are sap-suckers, such as aphids, capsid bugs, whitefly, or red spider mites (these are very tiny). Some insects, such as scale insects, are not mobile and look like small scales or mussels. Others, such as woolly aphids or mealy bugs, may be protected with a white cotton-wool-like covering.

Control: For difficult-to-control pests such as scale insects, woolly aphids, whitefly, and red spider mites, a systemic insecticide such as permethrin with heptenophos is likely to be the most effective. For the others, the choice is wide and includes fenitrothion, malathion, pirimiphos-methyl, and derris.

If the leaves are their normal colour but damaged or distorted, with no sign of insects on the surface of the leaf . . .

● If there are white or yellowish wandering tunnels within the leaf, the cause will be one of the leaf miner maggots.
Control: Spray with a contact insecticide such as HCH or a systemic such as dimethoate; if you want a 'natural' insecticide, you could use derris.

● If the leaves are spun together with a webb, possibly with holes in the leaves too, a tortrix moth caterpillar is the likely cause. A bad infestation of red spider mites will also cause webbing; look carefully to see the tiny mites.
Control: For tortrix moth caterpillars try permethrin with heptenophos (systemic). For red spider mites use a systemic such as dimethoate or a contact insecticide such as fenitrothion or malathion.

If the leaves are showing colour variations (other than natural variegation)

● Pale mottled flecks or patches suggest leafhoppers (look on the undersides – you may find small yellowish insects or their empty white skins). Pale, bronze-coloured leaves suggest a mite infestation, such as red spider mite. Look carefully for the tiny mites. The leaves may also be slightly contorted.
Control: For leafhoppers try any of the systemic insecticides, or a contact insecticide such as permethrin, pirimiphos-methyl, or pyrethrum. For red spider mites use a systemic such as dimethoate or a contact insecticide such as fenitrothion or malathion.

● Curled or distorted young leaves suggest the growing tip has been damaged by aphids, or an attack by a leaf-curling aphid.
Control: Use any of the systemic insecticides or a contact insecticide such as malathion, pirimicarb, pirimiphos-methyl, derris, or pyrethrum.

If there is some form of growth or mould on the leaves . . .

● A white growth is likely to be a mildew. If it is mealy or powdery-looking it is probably powdery mildew. This is most commonly found on the *upper* surface of the leaf, and is likely to be worst in hot, dry conditions. A white bloom is likely to be downy mildew which is most common on the *lower* surface of the leaf, and is likely to be worse in damp conditions.
Control: For powdery mildew try benomyl or thiophanate-methyl (both systemic). For downy mildew try a copper fungicide or mancozeb.

● A fluffy grey mould, sometimes giving off a cloud of dust-like spores if disturbed when dry, is likely to be botrytis (grey mould).
Control: Try benomyl, carbendazim, or thiophanate-methyl (all systemic).

● Black or brown blotches or spots, especially on roses, is likely to be one of the leaf spots (black spot is a common problem of roses).
Control: Try benomyl, carbendazim, thiophanate-methyl (all systemic), or mancozeb.

● Raised spots or pimples, usually yellow, orange, or brown, are likely to be caused by a fungus called rust. There are a few galls produced on trees such as oaks that could be confused with a disease such as rust, but these are unlikely to occur on ordinary garden plants.
Control: Try propiconazole, triforine with bupirimate (systemics), or mancozeb.

If the leaves are mottled, yellowish, or crinkled unnaturally . . .

● Yellowish leaves, either along the veins or between the veins, on an outdoor plant, are likely to be caused by a trace element deficiency (see page 68), though if accompanied by stunted growth or crinkled leaves, suspect a virus and destroy the plant.
Control: Try foliar feeding with a liquid fertilizer containing trace elements, or buy a sachet of trace elements (they may be sold as fritted trace elements), and use according to instructions. If the problem is nutritional, the plant should soon respond. If it does not, suspect a virus and destroy the plant.

● If the leaves are generally mottled or crinkled, a virus infection is a likely cause.
Control: It is best to destroy the plant; there is no cure, and leaving an infected plant will put others at risk as viruses can be transferred by sap-sucking insects such as aphids (or even on a knife if you are taking cuttings).

● Reddish blisters, sometimes large, are likely to be peach leaf curl (it can affect other members of the Prunus family as well as peaches).
Control: Try a copper-based fungicide.

Bud and Flower Problems

If flowers are malformed or eaten . . .

● If the flowers are lopsided, sap-sucking insects such as capsid bugs have probably damaged the buds.
Control: You need to act when you first see signs of damage on the leaves. Try dimethoate (systemic), or fenitrothion, HCH, or pirimiphos-methyl.

● Chewed or damaged petals, are probably caused by earwigs (they usually hide during the day, so you may not see them at work).
Control: Try shaking the flowers to dislodge any hiding pests. You can set traps by packing straw into upturned plant pots on garden canes, but the traps will have to be emptied regularly for this to be a useful control. Insecticides to try include carbaryl, fenitrothion, and HCH.

● Mottled petals, speckled silver, are usually a sign of thrips (unless bad weather is the cause). The thrips are tiny black flies about 2 to 3 mm (1/10 in) long.
Control: Most contact insecticides should control thrips, otherwise use a systemic such as dimethoate, or heptenophos with permethrin.

If the flowers are covered in mould . . .

● Botrytis (grey mould) can be a common problem if the weather is damp and humid.
Control: Try benomyl, carbendazim, or thiophanate-methyl (all systemic).

Friends not Foes

Most of the insects that you find in the garden do no harm. Some are even beneficial and help to control the pests. Bees are useful (though sometimes annoying) as they help to pollinate fruit as well as provide honey for their owner. Avoid spraying open flowers.

Ladybirds help to control aphids, scale insects, mealy bugs, thrips, and mites. The green lacewing (left) feeds on aphids.

There are many other beneficial insects including centipedes, ichneumon flies, hoverflies and many beetles.

Trouble at the Roots

If a plant looks unhealthy without any obvious cause, such as insects or diseases on the leaves, the problem may lie with the roots. If the leaves turn yellow and wilt, or if growth is stunted, suspect a root problem. If flowering-sized bulbs do not flower, grubs in the bulb may be the cause. A large plant such as a shrub is unlikely to be affected seriously enough to restrict growth; it is usually herbaceous plants,

bulbs, annuals, and vegetables that are the most likely to suffer from soil pests and diseases. These should be small enough to lift for examination if scraping a little soil away from the surface does not provide the answer. Bear in mind that sometimes the grubs may be *inside* the roots or the base of the stem.

● If larvae such as leatherjackets, wireworms, cutworms, chaffer grubs or vine weevils are found it is worth taking control measures.
Control: Disturbing the soil by hoeing regularly may help, but you really need to use a soil insecticide such as bromophos or diazinon.

● If there are tiny grubs in the roots or the base of the stem, they are likely to be the larvae of various flies (carrot fly, onion fly, cabbage root fly, for instance).
Control: Try a soil insecticide such as bromophos or diazinon. There are also non-chemical methods that you can try for some of the pests (see page 135).

● If the stem is severed, slugs, snails, or cutworms are likely to be the culprits.
Control: Use a slug bait based on metaldehyde or methiocarb. Cutworms are best controlled with a soil insecticide such as bromophos or diazinon.

Tubers, Bulbs, Corms

Always examine bulbs, corms, and tubers before you plant them. Any that are soft should be burned. However, you cannot always predict an infected bulb from the outside, and sometimes trouble is only obvious once the plant has started to grow. If bulbs are not growing well, lift one and examine it carefully (cut it open if necessary).

If you can see insects on the outside of the dry bulb . . .
Aphids are the most likely insects that you will find, especially on tulips and lilies, although they may be found on other kinds too. Unless you kill them, growth will probably be distorted.
Control: You can kill most of them by rubbing them off; dipping them in an insecticidal solution is more thorough.

If you find maggots in the bulb (you may have to cut it open) . . .
It is likely to be the grub of the narcissus fly. The bulb is likely to be soft or rotten, and the leaves few in number, and probably no flowers.
Control: Destroy affected bulbs because various rots will take over where the maggot has left off.

Understanding Fungicides

Fungus diseases are much more difficult to control than most pests, once they are established.

Most traditional fungicides are *protective*. They provide a barrier that prevents the spores infecting the plant but this means that their success depends on using them at the right time. They are no use once the disease is established. Fungicides of this type include mancozeb and those based on copper.

Even *curative* fungicides are only likely to stop an established infection

getting any worse and may not eliminate it completely. Most curative fungicides, such as benomyl and thiophanate-methyl, are systemic (they are absorbed by the plant and are then carried round to all parts in the sap).

Most fungicides are applied as sprays, but dusts are sometimes used on bulbs and tubers to be stored, and for applying as a seed dressing. Smoke cones are useful in the greenhouse, but of course are not used outdoors.

If the bulb is soft or mouldy, with no sign of insects or grubs . . .
Various fungi are likely to be responsible. It could also be caused by stem and bulb eelworms (if this is so, there are likely to be dark rings in the bulb when you cut it across; and there may be small yellow swellings on the pale, distorted leaves of the growing plant).
Control: Whatever the cause, it is best to destroy the affected bulbs. If one of the normal bulb rots seems to be responsible, take the precaution of dipping unaffected bulbs from the same batch or piece of ground in a fungicidal solution such as benomyl or thiophanate-methyl. If you suspect eelworm, do not plant bulbous plants on the affected ground for at least three years.

If there are black moulds or growths on the outside of the bulb . . .
One of the fungal diseases such as narcissus smoulder or tulip fire is likely to be responsible. Do not plant or store affected bulbs, and soak others from the same batch or area in a fungicidal solution such as benomyl when lifting and before planting.

The Chemicals Suggested

The chemicals recommended here may not be the only ones that will help to control a particular problem – there are, for instance, more than a dozen chemicals that you can buy to kill aphids, and many more if you count individual brands, but they are *examples* of the most effective ones. The order in which they are listed does not imply a preference.

Where the word 'with' occurs, this does not imply that you have to buy a second product – it means that the insecticide or fungicide is sold as a combined preparation.

It is a good idea to change the chemicals that you use periodically, to reduce the chance of resistant strains developing.

Always read the label carefully. Some of the products suggested may harm certain plants (sometimes at certain stages of growth), and not all are equally safe on food crops. The container should tell you the minimum interval to leave between treating and eating.

We have used common chemical names. Trade names may be different, but you will always find the name used here on the bottle, although sometimes in small print.

Alternatives to Insecticides

Not everyone likes using garden chemicals, especially among food crops, and there are alternatives for *some* pests.

General Principles
Garden hygiene makes sound sense, and will reduce the likelihood of some pests, whatever method of control you normally use. Tidy up the garden in autumn to reduce the hiding places in which pests can overwinter, and lift stumps and unused roots in the vegetable garden. If you grow a lot of just a few kinds of vegetables, rotate them each year if possible.

During the growing season, keep your eyes open. If you notice trouble early enough you can often pick off the affected leaf or nip out the shoot, and prevent it spreading. If caterpillars are few in number, hand picking may be as effective and as quick as mixing a spray.

Biological Control
In a greenhouse there are several useful methods of biological control, in which the pests are parasitized or eaten by the predator, but few of them are suitable for use outdoors in Britain. One biological control that will work outdoors is *Bacillus thuringiensis*, a bacterium that kills caterpillars without harming other insects. Buy a sachet of dried spores and mix the powder with water, then spray like an ordinary insecticide. When the caterpillars eat the sprayed leaves they become infected and die.

Understanding Insecticides

Most insecticides are *contact* insecticides – they kill by coming into contact with the pest when you spray or dust, or when pests eat the leaves contaminated with the chemical. These can be very effective, but make sure the plant is well covered: pay special attention to the undersides of the leaves when applying the insecticides, as many insects feed on the undersurface.

Systemic insecticides are absorbed by the plant and moved about in the sap. It means that it is less important to cover all parts of the plant. Systemics are especially effective at killing sap-sucking insects such as aphids, and they will reach insects that are usually well protected (scale insects, and any protected by rolled-up leaves for example).

Dusts are useful for fairly large crawling pests such as caterpillars and weevils. *Sprays* are better for pests that are likely to hide under or among the leaves. *Aerosols* do not really have a place in the garden, though they are useful in the greenhouse and home. Make sure they are safe for use indoors.

Granules are used against some soil pests. They can be formulated to release the insecticide slowly and are therefore usually long-lasting.

Barriers

Barriers can work surprisingly well. Collars placed around brassica stems are very effective. Buy them, or make them from circles of old carpet underlay (some proprietary ones may also be impregnated with an insecticide). They deter the cabbage root fly laying eggs at the base of the stem.

A barrier of clear plastic about 75 cm (2½ ft) high around newly-sown carrots (or a lower one round strawberries) can be effective in reducing the numbers of carrot flies and strawberry beetles respectively.

One of the oldest forms of barrier protection is the grease band – a strip of greased paper that is tied around the trunk of fruit trees to catch the wingless female winter moths as they climb the trees to lay their eggs. These are normally kept in place from November to February.

Traps

Slug traps are often advertized; they may catch some slugs, but the chances of eliminating a slug problem in this way is not great. Do not expect these to be the solution to a slug problem. Slugs are very destructive, especially in wet seasons. It is difficult to control them without using baits.

There are, however, modern, scientific traps for catching codling moths – the pests that lay eggs on young apples, which hatch into the maggots found later in the fruit. They are difficult to control with insecticides and the trees must be sprayed two or three times during the egg-laying period. These traps contain a pheromone, an artificial version of the scent the female moth produces to attract males. The male moths are attracted to the trap by the scent and come to a sticky end on the fly-paper type mat. With no males, the females cannot do much harm. If you have a lot of fruit trees, try using one trap to indicate when it is necessary to spray the other trees.

Weather Damage

Some plants die or look diseased simply as a reaction to the weather. If an evergreen becomes brown in winter or early spring, or the leaf tips turn brown or black, it is most likely to be due to cold or to drying winds (the wind causes moisture to be lost from the plant, but if the weather is cold the plant will not be able to take up water from the soil to replace it). In very cold weather, it is worth protecting valuable evergreens with some form of screen. Newly planted specimens should also be given special consideration.

Some plants with tender young foliage, such as *Acer palmatum* 'Dissectum', are easily scorched by cold spring winds and the edges of the leaves may shrivel.

If the ground is waterlogged, the leaves of some plants may turn yellow, and the plant even collapse.

Other Problems

It has not been possible here to mention all the pests and diseases that you might encounter. Usually, you will be able to tell whether it is an insect that is the problem. If it is obviously a fungus disease, try pruning out the worst affected part of the plant, and spray with a fungicide – a systemic fungicide is likely to be the best choice if you are unsure of the best one to use. This will be absorbed into the plant's sap and carried round to all parts of the plant.

If you can see neither insects nor signs of a fungal infection, and nothing is affecting the roots, yet the plant looks decidedly sick, treat the problem seriously. It could be a soil deficiency (see page 68), but it is much more likely to be due to a virus or to eelworms. Cut your losses and burn the plant.

Weed Control

Keeping weeds under control is more than just an aesthetic consideration, it also means that the other garden plants should grow better.

A decade or so ago weedkillers were seen mainly as a way of clearing neglected land, controlling lawn weeds, or perhaps keeping paths weed-free. Modern weedkillers can be used much more freely among vegetables, fruit and ornamental plants; and even if you want to clear a neglected area it is possible to kill difficult weeds and still use the land in a relatively short time.

Using weedkillers can be expensive, however, and used carelessly they can do a lot of harm, but do not overlook the contribution they can make to convenience gardening.

Using the right weedkiller at the right time will save hours of weeding; and if you are reclaiming a neglected area you can probably save yourself a season of work.

Which Weedkiller?

No one weedkiller is suitable for all situations – choose one that is suitable for the job. Suitable chemicals are suggested here; most are available from shops and garden centres, but a few may have to be bought by mail order. The common chemical name is used – this will always be written on the container, although trade names may be different.

To keep a path or drive weedfree . . .
Try aminotriazole + simazine (also available with paraquat + diquat to kill existing green foliage), or dichlobenil, or altrazine + aminotriazole.

To clear vacant ground . . .
If you want to clear vacant ground with no plants that you want to preserve, before cultivating or replanting try paraquat + diquat if you have mainly annual weeds and want to replant within days.

If you have difficult perennial weeds, and want to replant within weeks, try glyphosate.

If you can wait for 8 to 12 weeks before replanting, try ammonium sulphamate; or if you just want to control difficult grasses and can wait for 6–8 weeks before planting, consider dalapon.

To kill grass among non-grass plants . . .
Try alloxydim sodium.

To kill weeds around growing cultivated plants . . .
For annual weeds or light weed growth around established plants, try paraquat + diquat if you can be sure to keep the spray off the cultivated plants; or use dichlobenil (which is used in winter or early spring and will prevent new weed seedlings emerging for several months).

For difficult weeds around established plants, try painting the leaves of the weeds with glyphosate (but it will kill the desired plants just as readily if used carelessly).

To keep cleaned ground around shrubs weed-free, use propachlor (it will control emerging weeds for 6 to 8 weeks and is useful if you want to replant after a couple of months); or use simazine (the effect can last for a year).

To kill weeds in the lawn . . .
To kill lawn weeds use a selective weedkiller sold specifically for lawns.

For a just a few weeds, hand weeding may be as quick as mixing and using a weedkiller, and as effective. If you want to use a weedkiller and the weeds are few in number, spot weeding may be the answer.

For more numerous weeds use a lawn weedkiller that is sprayed or watered on, although time can be saved by using a combined weed-and-feed product.

If you have a particular problem weed, some weedkillers may be more suitable than others, but most modern lawn weedkillers contain a combination of chemicals that treat a wide variety of weeds. These are likely to control all lawn weeds if you persevere. Do not expect to kill them all with one application, some may need treating several times. It may be best to spot-treat the few remaining persistent weeds with a wipe-on stick.

Using Weedkillers
Always treat weedkillers with respect. Always wash out the watering-can or sprayer afterwards (ideally keep one just for weedkillers – a plastic can is better than a metal one, which may be affected by some weedkillers), and if possible use a dribble bar or shield to prevent spray drift.

Never apply a liquid weedkiller on a windy day. The consequences could be serious not only for your own garden, but for your neighbour's too.

Most modern path weedkillers should not 'creep' into the adjoining beds – but beware of using a liquid weedkiller on a sloping path or drive as surplus may run off into the flower beds.

Read the instructions carefully – not only for safety reasons, but to make sure the weedkiller will work properly. Timing is often important. With some the plants need to be growing actively, and it could be a waste of time if you apply them in winter for instance. Others should not be used if it is about to rain, some work best in sunny weather.

Do not be surprised if the weeds do not die immediately, however. Some weedkillers, such as glyphosate, have to be absorbed by the plant and translocated before they work. It may be a few weeks before the weeds die.

Alternatives to Weedkillers
If you do not use a weedkiller, hand weeding or hoeing is likely to be necessary initially. But once the ground is clear there are several ways in which weeds can be controlled.

Mulching is one of the most useful ways because organic mulches benefit the plants directly as well as reducing weed competition (see page 31). But if the mulch is to be effective at suppressing weeds it must be at least 5 cm (2 in) thick.

Black plastic film will also prevent weed growth, and it is well worth considering for use in the vegetable garden, for example.

You can buy squares of material to place around newly planted trees, and these are well worth considering as they reduce weed competition and help to conserve moisture too.

Hoeing is effective, but you must persevere if you have to control perennial weeds. Even difficult weeds will exhaust themselves eventually if the top growth is chopped off often enough – do not let the growth reach more than 5–10 cm (2–4 in) high.

Flame guns are all right for killing top growth and seeds on or close to the surface, but it is a slow job.

COMMON NAME INDEX

INDEX

Acknowledgements

The illustration on the contents page was photographed by S & O Mathews at Cobblers, Crowborough, East Sussex by kind permission of the owners Mr & Mrs Martin Furniss

Picture credits

Dr P. Becker: 132(1)
Steve Bicknell: 84, 87(t)
Pamela Booth: 63(br)
Pat Brindley: 30, 41, 64, 98, 103(t), 110, 112, 113, 117
R. J. Corbin: 127, 128, 134
Valerie Finnis: 62, 63(bl), 109
John Glover: 31, 96, 126
Derek Gould: 106
P. Hunt: 19
G. Hyde: 131(t,b)
J. Markham: 18, 38(l), 107
S & O Mathews: endpapers, contents, 8, 10, 34, 58, 66, 73, 74, 91, 94, 101, 118
Peter McHoy: 15(l,r), 23, 25, 43, 44, 45, 48, 49, 67, 77(b), 80, 95, 97, 125
Murphy Chemical Co: 130
Shell: 129, 132(r)
Miki Slingsby: 124
Harry Smith Horticultural Photographic Collection: 21, 29, 57, 59, 61(br), 71, 88, 105
Soil Survey of England and Wales: 12
Ron Sutherland: 120
Michael Warren: title page, 17, 27, 39, 53, 61(bl), 82, 92, 100, 103(b), 108, 111, 114, 116
Colin Watmough: 38(r)

Artwork

Eugene Fleury: 36, 37
Chris Forsey: 104
Richard Gliddon: 103
Hayward Art Group: 26, 32, 42(r), 46, 59(l), 66(l), 71, 72, 75, 76, 77, 78, 84(t), 90, 93
Aziz Khan: 13, 15, 16, 28, 33, 47, 58, 79, 81, 121, 122, 123, 127
Kevin Maddison: 40, 42(l), 51, 86
Coral Mula: 87
Michael Woods: 22, 25, 50, 54, 56(l)